C000039280

THE JUNGLE

by Joe Murphy
and Joe Robertson

The Jungle premiered as a co-production between
Young Vic and the National Theatre with Good Chance Theatre,
commissioned by the National Theatre.

It opened at the Young Vic on 7 December 2017

Henri/Yasin	**Raphael Acloque**
Amal	**Aliya Ali**
	Alyssa Denise D'Souza
Norullah	**Mohammad Amiri**
Muzamil	**Elham Ehsas**
Boxer	**Trevor Fox**
Omid	**Moein Ghobsheh**
Derek	**Michael Gould**
Safi	**Ammar Haj Ahmad**
Mohammed	**Ansu Kabia**
Yohannes	**Bruk Kumelay**
Sam	**Alex Lawther**
Paula	**Jo McInnes**
Okot	**John Pfumojena**
Beth	**Rachel Redford**
Ali	**Rachid Sabitri**
Omar	**Mohamed Sarrar**
Salar	**Ben Turner**
Helene	**Nahel Tzegai**
Direction	**Stephen Daldry**
	& Justin Martin
Design	**Miriam Buether**
Costume	**Catherine Kodicek**
Light	**Jon Clark**
Sound	**Paul Arditti**
Composer and	
Musical Direction	**John Pfumojena**
Video	**Tristan Shepherd**
Casting	**Julia Horan, CDG**
Dialect	**Zabarjad 'Budgie' Salam**
Fights	**Terry King**
Voice	**Jeannette Nelson**
Creative Consultant	**Amy Reade**
Assistant Director	**Nicole Charles**
Design Assistant	**Joana Dias**

Nicole Charles is supported by the Jerwood
Assistant Directors Programme at the Young Vic

Video Producer	**Tamara Moore**
Archive Research	**Belinda Harris**
Production Manager	**Anthony Newton**
Stage Manager	**Jane Suffling**
Deputy Stage Manager	**Georgia Bird**
Assistant Stage Manager	**Francesca Reidy**
Assistant Stage Manager (Props)	**Kareen Thomas**
Costume Supervisor	**Jackie Orton**
Lighting Operator	**Nick Di Gravio**
Sound Operator	**Bryony Blackler**
Automation Operator	**Sam Shuck**
Stage Crew	**Sam Palmer**
Wardrobe Manager	**Florence McGlynn**
Make Up	**Natalia Osipova**
Special Effects Make Up	**Sam Shuck**
Breaking Down	**Gabrielle Firth**
Laundry Maintenance	**Rachel Welch**
Video Programmer	**Dan Barnicott**
Scenic Drafting	**Tom Atkinson**
	Emma Hayward
Armourer	**Paul Wanklin**
Scenic Art	**The National Theatre Workshops**
Production Assistant Stage Management Work Placement	**Kady Howey Nunn**
	Kenzie Murray
Set built by	**The Young Vic and National Theatre workshops**
Good Chance Ensemble Manager	**Amy Reade**
Chaperone	**Valerie Joyce**
Food supplied by	**The Cut Bar**

The Jungle is generously supported by
Clive and Sally Sherling and Glenn and Phyllida Earle.

Good Chance Theatre are supported by
The KT Wong Foundation.

The Young Vic 2017 season is generously supported
by the Garfield Weston Foundation, Genesis Foundation,
The Richenthal Foundation, The Sackler Trust
and an anonymous donor.

We would like to thank
Emma Jones, Majid Adin, Steve Colley,
Andrew Ormersher, Dagmar Ulrich, Paul Hornsby,
Giuseppe Cannas, National Theatre Props and
Costume Hire, Erica Campayne.

Special thanks to Conor Neaves

RAPHAEL ACLOQUE | Henri/Yasin

Theatre includes: *As You Like It, Rabbit, Fast Labour, Nell Gwyn, Macbeth, Hindle Wakes, The Lady's Tragedy, The Rivals, Death and the Maiden, The Comedy of Errors, The Duchess of Malfi* (LAMDA).

Television includes: *24: Legacy, Knightfall, Humans, Tyrant, The Secret Agent.*

Film includes: *Allied, Burnt, The Danish Girl.*

ALIYA ALI | Amal

Theatre includes*: A Tale Of Two Cities* (Regent's Park Open Air Theatre).

Opera includes: *The Pearl Fishers* (ENO).

Television includes: *Damned, Eastenders.*

MOHAMMAD AMIRI | Norullah

Theatre includes: *Boy* (Almeida).

Television includes: *Unforgotten 2.*

Film includes: *Fighting With My Family, City of Tiny Lights.*

ALYSSA DENISE D'SOUZA | Amal

Training: BKD Performers.

ELHAM EHSAS | Muzamil

Film includes: *The Kill Team, Oksijan, War Machine, Kite Runner.*

Television includes: *The Informer, Brussel, Silent Witness.*

TREVOR FOX | Boxer

Theatre includes: *People Places and Things* (UK tour), *Common* (National Theatre), *Billy Elliot, The Curious Incident of the Dog In The Night-Time* (West End); *The Pitman Painters* (National Theatre/New York); *The Tempest, Cymbeline, The Oresteia, Measure for Measure, A Midsummer Night's Dream* (Globe); *Children's Children, King Lear* (Almeida); *Your Home in the West, Toast* (Live Theatre, Newcastle).

Television includes: *The Moonstone, Joe Maddison's War, The Walk, Our Friends In The North.*

Film includes: *Bridget Jones – The Edge Of Reason, Billy Elliot.*

MOEIN GHOBSHEH | Omid

Milan is a musician from Iran. This is his U.K. theatrical debut.

Music includes: *Manoto Stage.*

MICHAEL GOULD | Derek

Young Vic includes: *A Midsummer Night's Dream*, *A View from the Bridge* (also West End/Broadway), *Hamlet, Cruel and Tender.*

Other theatre includes: *Waves, Women of Troy, Earthquakes in London, Our Class* (National); *The Audience* (Apollo); *The Ugly One* (Royal Court); *Othello* (RSC); King Lear (Shakespeare's Globe).

Television includes: *Man Down, The Trial, Decline and Fall, The Bletchley Circle, Silent Witness, Wallander.*

Film includes: *Darkest Hour, Rogue One, Our Kind of Traitor, Crocodile, Private Peaceful, Room 8* (BAFTA Best Short).

AMMAR HAJ AHMAD | Safi

Theatre includes: *LOVE* (National Theatre/Birmingham Rep); *The Great Survey of Hastings* (Ladies' Parlour); *Goats/Told From the Inside* (Royal Court); *Kan Yama* (Cockpit Theatre); *Mawlana* (Mosaic Rooms); *The Knight and the Crescent Hare* (UK tour); *Babel* (Caledonian Park); *One Thousand and One Nights* (The Joey and Toby Tanenbaum Opera Centre, Toronto/Lyceum Theatre, Edinburgh).

Television includes: *Agatha Raisin, Letters from Baghdad*, plus many other Arabic television credits.

Film includes: *London Tomorrow, ALEGNA, Wall, Round Trip, Maqha Almawt, Wada'an, Monologue.*

ANSU KABIA | Mohammed

Theatre includes: *Hamlet* (RADA), *Romeo and Juliet, Harlequinade, The Winter's Tale* (Garrick); *To Sir with Love* (Royal & Derngate/tour); *The Merry Wives of Windsor, The Mouse and His Child, Mojo, Little Eagles, Antony and Cleopatra, King Lear, As You Like It* (RSC); *She Rode Horses Like the Stock Exchange* (Old Vic), *A Few Man Fridays* (Cardboard Citizens).

Television includes: *Wizards vs Aliens, London's Burning, Utopia, The Bill, Ten Days to War, Casualty*

Film includes: *Murder on the Orient Express*

BRUK KUMELAY | Yohannes

This is Bruk's UK theatrical debut.

Theatre includes: *Hope Shows* (Good Chance Calais).

ALEX LAWTHER | Sam

Theatre includes: *Crushed Shells and Mud* (Southwark Playhouse); *The Glass Supper*, *Fault Lines* (Hampstead Theatre); *South Downs* (Harold Pinter/Chichester).

Television includes: *The End of the Fucking World, Howard's End, Black Mirror.*

Film includes: *Ghost Stories, Goodbye Christoper Robin, Freak Show, Old Boys, Departure* (winner, Best Actor – Dublin International Film Festival); *The Imitation Game* (winner, Young British Performer – London Film Critics' Circle), *X+Y*.

JO McINNES | Paula

Theatre includes: *Wastewater, Fleshwound, Bluebird, 4.48 Psychosis* (Royal Court); *The House of Bernarda Alba, The Children's Hour* (National Theatre); *On Blindness, dirty butterfly* (Soho Theatre).

Television includes: *Eternal Law, Five Daughters, Material Girl, Recovery, Afterlife, Sorted, The World of Impressionists, Spooks, Living It, Playing the Field*.

Film includes: *Me and Orson Welles, The New Romantics, My Wife is an Actress, Birthday Girl, Gangster No. 1.*

Jo also works extensively as a director.

JOHN PFUMOJENA | Okot / Composer and Musical Direction

Theatre includes: *Bent, Peter Pan* (National Theatre); *Twelfth Night* (Shakespeare's Globe); *Workshop Negative* (The Gate); *I Am Thomas* (National Theatre of Scotland); *Beasty Baby* (Theatre Rights/Polka Theatre); *Now You See Me* (Immediate Theatre); *The Maids* (Zimbabwe tour); *Water, Bread and Salt* (Tangle Café and UK tour); *Dream Nation* (UK tour); *Much Ado About Nothing* (Reps Theatre Zimbabwe); *The Coup, Waiting for Constitution* (Theatre in the Park, Zimbabwe), *Diary of a Madman* (Spear Theatre Zimbabwe).

RACHEL REDFORD | Beth

Theatre includes: *The Crucible* (Manchester Royal Exchange); *Luna Gale* (Hampstead Theatre); *Closer* (Donmar Warehouse); *A Ghost from a Perfect Place* (Arcola); *Adler and Gibb* (Royal Court); *Not The Worst Place* (Sherman Theatre/ Theatr Clwyd); *Parallel Lines* (Chapter Arts Centre); *A Family Affair* (Sherman Theatre); *The Acid Test, Blue Stockings, King Lear* (RADA); *Romeo and Juliet* (The Gate, Cardiff).

Television includes: *Gap Year.*

Film includes: *Testament of Youth, The Riot Club, Nights.*

RACHID SABITRI | Ali

Theatre includes: *Aladdin* (West End); *Romeo and Juliet* (West End); *I Call My Brothers* (Off Broadway and Arcola); *Twelfth Night* (Westport Country Playhouse and Northampton Theatre Royal); *Rafta Rafta* (Old Globe, San Diego; National Theatre UK tour); *The Tale of the Allergists Wife* (La Marida Playhouse, LA).

Television includes: *Homeland, Criminal Minds, Madam Secretary, Generation Kill, Dr Who, The Odds, The Walk, Wannabes, The Bill, Casualty, Family Business, Blue Murder.*

Radio includes: *Silver Street, Together.*

MOHAMED SARRAR | Omar

Mohamed is a musician from Sudan. He has been in the UK for two years.

Theatre includes: *The Welcoming Party* (Theatre Rights International Festival, Manchester); *Encampment* (Southbank Centre); *Hope Shows* (Good Chance Calais).

As part of the theatre ensemble Psyche Delight, Mohamed has toured internationally performing the show *Borderline* at The Cockpit, Brighton Fringe Festival, the Migration Museum in London, Migrants Matter in Sheffield, Platforma Arts in Newcastle and Stockton, Freedom of Movement Festival in Berlin, Action Moon Star in Black Forest Germany, Bridewell Theatre in London and in the upcoming Tenth International Theatre Festival of Kerala in India.

BEN TURNER | Salar

Young Vic includes: *Soldier's Fortune.*

Theatre includes: *The Kite Runner, As You Like It* (Wynham's Theatre/ UK tour); *The Iliad* (Royal Lyceum Theatre); *Maiden Voices from the Uprising* (Royal Court); *Richard II, Caligula* (Donmar Warehouse); *Awake and Sing* (Almeida); *Measure For Measure/Habeus Corpus* (tour); *The Merchant of Venice* (RSC / tour).

Television includes: *The Coroner, WPC 56, Death In Paradise, Casualty, The Bill, Dr Who, Love Soup.*

Film includes: *Six Days, 300: Rise of an Empire, The Fifth Estate, Adulthood, Syriana.*

NAHEL TZEGAI | Helene

Theatre includes: *How It Ended* (Bush Theatre); *Ring* (BAC); *The Ship's Name* (Royal Court); *You Are Currently the Highest Bidder, Block 9, Virtually Real* (Roundhouse); *Isilwanyana Esoyikekayo* (Trinity College).

Radio includes: *Black Dog, Cuttin' It* and *The Brave Little Tailor.*

JOE MURPHY & JOE ROBERTSON

Joe Murphy grew up in Leeds and Joe Robertson grew up in Hull. They began writing plays together at university in 2011. Their short plays include *Fairway Manor* (Burton Taylor Studio, Oxford Playhouse), *Ten Bits on Boondoggling* and *Paper Play* (Edinburgh Fringe) and *Maria Popova* (Greater Manchester tram network).

In 2015, they established Good Chance Theatre in the 'Jungle' refugee and migrant camp in Calais, a space of expression where theatre, art, dance and music could be made. They lived there for seven months until the eviction of the southern half of the camp. In 2016, Good Chance built its original Calais theatre in view of the UK Parliament for *Encampment,* a major festival at Southbank Centre in London, with a programme of 110 artists from around the world, run by former residents of the camp. Good Chance then began working in Paris with theatres, humanitarian organisations and local communities to create new spaces of expression, welcome and introductions. In January 2018, two new temporary theatres of hope will be built in the north of Paris.

The Jungle is Joe and Joe's first full-length play.

STEPHEN DALDRY | Direction

Stephen started his career at the Sheffield Crucible Theatre and directed extensively in Britain's regional theatres. In London he was Artistic Director of the Gate Theatre and the Royal Court Theatre where he headed the £26million redevelopment. He has also directed at the National Theatre, the Public Theatre in New York and transferred many productions both to Broadway and the West End. His award-winning 1992 National Theatre production of *An Inspector Calls* recently completed a sixteen-week run in the West End following a successful UK tour. *Billy Elliot the Musical* opened at the Victoria Palace Theatre in 2005 and ran for eleven years. It recently finished a highly successful eighteen-month tour of the UK and Ireland. It has also played on Broadway, in Hamburg, Holland, Seoul, Sydney, Melbourne, Chicago, Toronto and the US. It is currently running in Tokyo with a further production opening in Korea in December 2017. In 2009, the production won ten Tony awards including Best Musical, more than any other British show in Broadway history. Stephen's first four films, *Billy Elliot, The Hours, The Reader* and *Extremely Loud and Incredibly Close,* together received nineteen Academy Award nominations and two wins. His film *Trash* was nominated for a 2015 BAFTA for Best Film Not in the English Language. He also directed *The Audience* and *Skylight* to critical acclaim both in London and on Broadway. Stephen has directed for BBC Radio and television. He is Executive Producer and Director of the highly acclaimed award-winning Netflix series *The Crown* by Peter Morgan, which won Best Drama Series at the Golden Globes. Stephen was Creative Executive Producer of the Opening and Closing Ceremonies for the London 2012 Olympic and Paralympic Games. He is Chairman of Good Chance Theatre, working with refugees, Co-Director of Pier 55 in New York, and also on the Board of the Perelman Arts Center at the World Trade Center in New York.

JUSTIN MARTIN | Direction

Justin Martin previously directed *Last Chance* with Good Chance Theatre at the Young Vic in 2016.

Theatre includes: *Low Level Panic* (Old Fitz Theatre, Sydney; Galway Theatre Festival and Irish national tour), *Street* (Mick Laly Theatre), *The Black Balloon* (in development); *Harvey and Frieda* (Arcola Theatre); *Far Away* and *Skintight* (fortyfivedownstairs, Melbourne); *The Kitchen* (HMS Theatre, Vic), *Echarcissus* (Natya Mandala Theatre); and *Billie* (The Studio, Sydney Opera House and La Mama). As Associate Director: *The Inheritance* (workshop); *Skylight, The Audience* (West End, Broadway); *Let the Right One In* (National Theatre of Scotland,Royal Court, Apollo Theatre, St Anne's Warehouse), *Billy Elliot* (New York, Toronto, Brazil, Chicago, North America tour, Korea and Australia); and *The Give and Take* (Sydney Theatre Company, Melbourne Theatre Company).

Television includes: *The Crown*.

MIRIAM BUETHER | Design

Young Vic includes: *The Trial, Measure for Measure, Public Enemy, Wild Swans, The Government Inspector, In the Red and Brown Water, The Good Soul of Szechuan* and *Generations*.

Other theatre includes: *A Doll's House 2* (Broadway); *Escaped Alone* (BAM); *Sunny Afternoon, Chariots of Fire* (Hampstead Theatre/West End); *Wild* (Hampstead Theatre); *In the Republic of Happiness, Love* and Information (also New York), *Sucker Punch*, *Cock*, *My Child* (Royal Court); *Bend it Like Beckham* (West End); *The Father* (Theatre Royal Bath); *Albion, Boy, Game, When the Rain Stops Falling, Judgement Day* (Almeida); *The Effect, Earthquakes in London* (National Theatre); *Decade* (Headlong); *King Lear* (New York); *Six Characters in Search of an Author* (Chichester Festival Theatre/West End); *Everybody Loves a Winner* (Manchester International Festival); *The Wonderful World of Dissocia* (Edinburgh International Festival/Royal Court); *trade* (RSC/Soho Theatre); *Guantanamo: 'Honor Bound to Defend Freedom'* (Tricycle Theatre/West End/US tour).

CATHERINE KODICEK | Costumes

Catherine is currently Head of Costume at the Young Vic.

Previous Young Vic: *Life of Galileo, A Midsummer Night's Dream, A View from the Bridge* (also West End), *Yerma, Once in a Lifetime, The Scottsboro Boys* (also West End), *The Changeling, Measure for Measure, A Season in the Congo, Blackta* (all as Costume Supervisor).

JON CLARK | Light

Previous Young Vic: *Life of Galileo, A Streetcar Named Desire* (also New York), *A Season in the Congo, Cat on a Hot Tin Roof* (at Apollo Theatre).

Other theatre includes: *Amadeus, As You Like It, The Beaux' Stratagem, Hamlet, Othello, The Effect, Our Class, The Cat in the Hat, Beauty and the Beast, Hansel and Gretel* (NT); *Hamlet, The Tempest, The Comedy of Errors, Twelfth Night, King Lear* (RSC); *Fatherland* (MIF); *Doctor Faustus, Made in Dagenham, The Commitments, I Can't Sing!, The Ruling Class, Three Days of Rain* (West End); *Richard III, King Charles III* (also West End and Broadway), *King Lear* (all Almeida); *Limehouse* (Donmar); *Tipping the Velvet* (Lyric Hammersmith); *Into the Woods* (Regent's Park).

Recent Opera includes: *The Exterminating Angel* (ROH, Salzburg and the Met); *Written on Skin* (ROH, Aix-en-Provence, Moscow, New York); *Hamlet* (Glyndebourne); *A Winter's Tale* (ENO and Amsterdam).

PAUL ARDITTI | Sound

Young Vic includes: *The Emperor* (also HOME Manchester); *A Midsummer Night's Dream, If You Kiss Me Kiss Me, A Streetcar Named Desire* (also Broadway); *The Scottsboro Boys* (also West End).

Recent theatre includes: *Labour of Love* (Noël Coward); *Young Marx* (Bridge Theatre); *Hamlet* (RADA); *Caroline or Change* (Chichester Festival Theatre); *Beginning, Mosquitoes, Amadeus* (Olivier nomination for Best Sound Design 2017), *The Threepenny Opera, wonder.land, Ma Rainey's Black Bottom, London Road* (National Theatre); *Mary Stuart, Bacchae, American Psycho* (Almeida); *King Charles III* (Almeida/West End/UK tour/Broadway); *The Glass Menagerie* (EIF/West End); *Charlie and the Chocolate Factory* (West End).

Awards include: Olivier, Tony and Drama Desk Awards for *Billy Elliot the Musical*; Olivier Award for *St Joan*; Evening Standard award for *Festen*; Drama Desk Award for *The Pillowman* and *Four Baboons Adoring the Sun*; Tony nominations for *Mary Stuart* and *One Man Two Guvnors*.

Paul is an associate at the National Theatre.

TRISTAN SHEPHERD | Video

Tristan is an award-winning filmmaker, who predominately works in theatre content and narrative fiction film. He co-founded the production company Take Cover Films in 2012.

Young Vic includes: *The Roof, Astoria* (both short films), *Life of Galileo, Cat on a Hot Tin Roof* (at Apollo Theatre), *Wings, Cuttin' It, Why Its Kicking Off Everywhere* (all trailers).

Other theatre includes: *Motown the Musical* (Shaftesbury Theatre); *Hairspray* (UK tour); *The Royale* (Bush); *Boy Will Be Boys* (Headlong/Bush); and *Crazy for You* (UK tour).

Other short film includes: *The Outside In and Among Sweet Flowers and Shades*.

JULIA HORAN CDG | Casting

Julia is an Associate Artist at the Young Vic.

Young Vic includes: *Cat on a Hot Tin Roof* (at Apollo Theatre), *Wings, Why It's Kicking Off Everywhere, Life of Galileo, Once in a Lifetime, Yerma, Blue/Orange, The Trial, Ah, Wilderness!, Happy Days, A View from the Bridge*(also Wyndham's/New York), *Public Enemy, The Shawl, Blackta, A Doll's House* (also Duke of York's/BAM), *The Events* (also ATC), *Wild Swans* (also ART).

Other theatre includes: *Harry Potter and the Cursed Child* (Palace); *Obsession, Hamlet* (Barbican); *The Treatment, Hamlet* (also Harold

Pinter); *Mary Stuart, Oil, Uncle Vanya, Medea, Oresteia* (also Trafalgar Studios), *Game, Mr Burns, Chimerica* (also Harold Pinter) (Almeida); *Hope, Teh Internet Is Serious Business, The Nether* (also Duke of York's), *Adler and Gibb, Birdland, Khandan, The Mistress Contract, The Pass, Wastwater, Tribes, Clybourne Park* (also Wyndham's); S*pur of the Moment, Sucker Punch* (all Royal Court); *The Lighthouse Keeper* (BCMG); *Red Velvet* (Tricycle/St Ann's Warehouse/Garrick); *Gaddafi* (ENO).

Film and television includes: *The Exception, Departure, The Trial: A Murder in the Family*

ZABARJAD 'BUDGIE' SALAM | Dialect

Young Vic includes: *The Island, Sizwe Bansi is Dead.*

Other theatre includes: *The Resistible Rise of Arturo Ui* (Donmar); *Flowers For Mrs Harris* (Crucible, Sheffield); *Ross* (Chichester Festival Theatre); *Future Conditional, The Mentalists* (Old Vic); *Cat on a Hot Tin Roof* (Theatre Clwyd); *Dinner with Saddam* (Menier Chocolate Factory); *The Winter's Tale, Liberian Girl* (Royal Court); *Who's Afraid of Virginia Woolf, Speed the Plow, Hay Fever* (Theatre Royal Bath); *Matilda, Julius Caesar, Empress* (RSC); *Let it Be* (Prince of Wales); *The Commitments* (Palace); *Harvey* (Theatre Royal Bath and tour); *Comedy of Errors, Travelling Light, Behind the Beautiful Forevers* (National Theatre); *Bend it Like Beckham* (Phoenix Theatre).

Film includes: *Caravan, The Dark Tower, Robin Hood Origins, Halal Daddy, Allied, The Conjuring 2, Lies We Tell, Jungle Book, Tulip Fever*

Television and radio includes: *Jamestown, Victoria, Gunpowder, Fighting With My Family, The ABC, Game of Thrones, Guerrilla, Black Mirror, Tutankhamun, Cilla, Indian Summers, Eden, The Missing.*

TERRY KING | Fights

Theatre credits: *His Dark Materials, Henry IV Parts I and II, Scenes from the Big Picture, Othello and The Duchess of Malfi (National Theatre); Hamlet, Henry VI, As You Like It, Macbeth, Romeo and Juliet, Twelfth Night and Cymbeline (RSC); Shakespeare in Love* (Globe).

Opera credits: *Porgy and Bess, Macbeth, Don Carlo, Troilus and Cressida.*

JEANNETTE NELSON | Voice

Jeannette Nelson is Head of Voice at the National Theatre. She has worked extensively as a voice coach in theatre, film and television. Besides the National Theatre she has been resident voice coach at Shakespeare's Globe, the Royal Shakespeare Company and Sydney Theatre Company, Australia.

Her other work in British theatre includes productions for the Royal Court, Donmar, Young Vic, Out of Joint, Shared Experience, Theatre de Complicite, Hampstead Theatre, English Touring Theatre, Sheffield Crucible Theatre, Birmingham Rep, Chichester Festival Theatre, Liverpool Playhouse, Salisbury Playhouse, Bristol Old Vic and many West End theatres.

Film includes: *The Merchant of Venice*, *Kingdom of Heaven*, *Wuthering Heights.*

Recent television includes: *The Hollow Crown.*

Her book *The Voice Exercise Book* is published by the National Theatre.

AMY READE | Creative Consultant & Good Chance Ensemble Manager

Amy ran Good Chance Theatre in Calais and is currently Artistic Associate at Good Chance. She is also President of the UCL Drama Society.

Young Vic includes: *Last Chance* (for Good Chance).

Other theatre includes: *Calai*s, *Pari*s, *Encampment* (Southbank Centre for Good Chance); *Pirates* (R&D, National Theatre as Assistant Director), *Walls* (Edinburgh Festival Fringe as writer and producer)

NICOLE CHARLES | Assistant Director

Young Vic includes: *Flashes* (Taking Part Parallel Production).

Theatre includes: as director, *Thanks for Coming* (Bush), *Forty Walls and Ten Doors* (site specific); as assistant director, *The Goat or*, *Who is Sylvia?* (Theatre Royal Haymarket); *Imogen*, *Love's Pilgrimage* (Shakespeare's Globe); *The Pirate Project* (UK tour).

JERWOOD **CHARITABLE** FOUNDATION

About The Young Vic

Our shows

We present the widest variety of classics, new plays, forgotten works and music theatre. We tour and co-produce extensively within the UK and internationally.

Our artists

Our shows are created by some of the world's great theatre people, alongside the most adventurous of the younger generation. This fusion makes the Young Vic one of the most exciting theatres in the world.

Our audience

. . . is famously the youngest and most diverse in London. We encourage those who don't think theatre is 'for them' to make it part of their lives. We give 10% of our tickets to schools and neighbours irrespective of box-office demand, and keep prices low.

Our partners near at hand

Each year we engage with over 11,000 local people – individuals and groups of all kinds including schools and colleges – by exploring theatre on and off stage. From time to time we invite our neighbours to appear on our stage alongside professionals.

Our partners further away

By co-producing with leading theatre, opera, and dance companies from London and around the world we create shows neither partner could achieve alone.

The hottest incubator of revitalized classics in London'
The New York Times

'The Young Vic is where theatre magic happens'
Time Out

'Cool, creative, edgy Young Vic'
iNews

'London's most essential theatre'
The Guardian

'Young Vic is London's most lovable theatre. The building welcomes; the programming dares. It offers danger in a safe place'
The Observer

The Young Vic is a company limited by guarantee, registered in England No. 1188209

VAT registration No. 236 673 348

The Young Vic (registered charity number No. 268876) receives public funding from:

Get more from the Young Vic online

 /youngvictheatre

 @youngvictheatre

 /youngviclondon

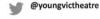 youngviclondon.wordpress.com

 /youngvictheatre

Sign up to receive email updates at
youngvic.org/register

The Young Vic Company

Artistic Director
David Lan
Executive Director
Lucy Woollatt

Associate Artistic
Director
Sue Emmas
Lead Producer
Daisy Heath
Producer
Ben Cooper

ASSOCIATES
Associate Designer
Jeremy Herbert
Associate Artists
Joe Hill-Gibbins
Julia Horan
Ian MacNeil
Sacha Wares
International
Associates
Benedict Andrews
Gísli Örn Gardarsson
Amir Nizar Zuabi
Associate
Companies
Belarus Free Theatre
BirdGang
Good Chance Theatre
Regional Theatre Young Directors Scheme

ADMINISTRATION
Director of IT and
Administration
Rathi Kumar
Assistant Producer
Iain Goosey
Data and Systems
Manager
Alex Fisher
Administrator to
the Producers
Tamara Moore

Assistant to the
Artistic Director
Andrew Hughes

DEVELOPMENT
Director of
Development and
Future Partnerships
Livvy Brinson
Development
Manager
Georgina Landau
Reed Nykiforuk
Natasha Ratter
Development
Officer
Éimear Doherty
Development
Assistant
Nick Hafezi

FINANCE
Finance Manager
Sophie Wells
Finance and
Contracts Assistant
Janine Carter

FRONT OF HOUSE
Theatre Manager
Paul Marshall
Front of House
Manager
Will Bowden
Operations
Assistant
Josh Husslebee
Duty Managers
Martin Dickinson
Megan Griffith
Claire Harris
Rosa Manzi-Reid
Chris Stevens
Maryam Shofowora
Boris Van Der Ree
Ushers
Joseph Ackerman
Simone Bell
Debbie Burningham
Oliver Byng
Morgyn Cliff
Laura Day
Francesca De Sica
Eboni Dixon
Sile Edwards
Patrick Elue
Tom Hadrill

Susan Harrold
Owen Haslegrave
William Heslop
Jessica James
Toheeb Jimoh
Grace Kayibanda
Aaron Kelly
Lynn Knight
George Mills
Glenn Mortimer
Taz Munyaneza
Sheila Murphy
Tobi Oludipe
Julie Patten
Luke Pierre
Gracjana Rejmer-Canovas
Thea Sandall
Joanna Selcott
Paula Shaw
Jack Sturt
Mark Vanderstoop
Isaac Vincent
Annette Williams
Eve Williams
Dan Young
Young Associate
Anthony Bloomfield

MARKETING AND PRESS
Director of
Marketing and
Press
Stacy Coyne
Marketing
Manager
Kyle Bradshaw
Press Manager
Sophie Wilkinson
Digital Manager
Leon Puplett
Ticketing Manager
Zoe Fitzpatrick
Marketing Officer
Lucy Gilham
Press and
Publications
Assistant
Christine Achampong
Young Associate
Lanikai Krishnadasan Torrens

PRODUCTION
Technical Director
Stuart Robertson
Company Manager
Jenny Grand
Head of Stage
Hilary Williamson
Head of Lighting
Sam McLeod
Head of Costume
Catherine Kodicek
Head of Sound
Peter Rice
Production
Manager
Sarah O'Connor
Production
Manager (Studios)
Tom Horton
Workshop Manager
Emma Hayward
Senior Sound
Technician
Bryony Blackler
Acting Senior
Lighting Technician
Jess Glaisher
Senior Stage
Technician
Craig Tye
Senior Costume
Technician
Kinnetia Isidore
Lighting Technician
Nick Di Gravio
Stage Technician
Ryan Smalley
Studio Technician
Nell Allen
Workshop
Carpenter
Ally Friedman
Production
Administrator
Rachel Salenius
Young Associate
Sandra Falase

TAKING PART
Director of Taking
Part
Imogen Brodie
Schools and
Colleges
Project Manager
Georgia Dale

Participation
Project Manager
Rob Lehmann
Two Boroughs &
Directors Program
Project Manager
Kirsten Adam
Two Boroughs
Projects Manager
Lily Einhorn
Taking Part
Assistant
Daniel Harrison
Young Associate
Patrick Ellis

WELCOME TEAM
Welcome Team
Manager
Ciara O'Toole
Welcome Team
Johanna Keane
Mariko Primarolo
Oliver Turner
Di Ypma

BOARD
Patrick McKenna
(Chair)
Nicky Dunn
Robert Easton
Sean Egan
David Fletcher
Rory Kinnear
Ali Hossaini
David Lan
Anna Lane
Ivan Lewis MP
Fiona Shaw
Rita Skinner
Steve Tompkins
Anna Williams

DEVELOPMENT BOARD
Rita Skinner
(Chair)
Beatrice Bondy
Caroline Cormack
Annabel Duncan-Smith
Sophie Hale
Anna Lane
Jill Manson
Will Meldrum
Chris Organ
Barbara Reeves
Magnus Scadden
Mark Selby

Supporting The Young Vic

To produce our sell-out, award-winning shows and provide thousands of free activities through our Taking Part programme requires major investment. Find out how you can make a difference and get involved.

As an individual . . . become a Friend, donate to a special project, attend our unique gala events or remember the Young Vic in your will.

As a company . . . take advantage of our flexible memberships, exciting sponsorship opportunities, corporate workshops, CSR engagement and venue hire. As a trust or foundation... support our innovative and forward-thinking programmes on stage and off.

As a trust and foundation... support our innovative and forward-thinking programmes on stage and off.

Are you interested in events... hire a space in our award-winning building and we can work with you to create truly memorable workshops, conferences or parties.

For more information visit **youngvic.org/support us** 020 7922 2810 Registered charity (No. 268876)

BackstageTrust

Garfield Weston

phf Paul Hamlyn Foundation

The Young Vic relies on the generous support of many individuals, trusts and foundations, and companies to produce our work, on and off stage. For their recent support we thank:

Public Funders
Arts Council England
Big Lottery Fund
British Council
Creative & Cultural Skills
Lambeth Borough Council
Southwark Council

Corporate Partners
American Express
Barclays
Bloomberg
IHS Markit
Wahaca

Corporate Members
aka
Bloomberg
Finsbury
Ingenious Media Plc
Memery Crystal
Royal Bank of Scotland
NatWest

Upper Circle
Lionel Barber and Victoria Greenwood
Sarah Billinghurst Solomon
Tony and Gisela Bloom
Simon and Sally Borrows
Sara Bunting
Sandra Cavlov
Ian and Caroline Cormack
Manfred and Lydia Gorvy
Patrick Handley
Jack and Linda Keenan
Adam Kenwright
Patrick McKenna
Sarah and Dominic Murphy

Simon and Midge Palley
Karl-Johan Persson
Barbara Reeves
Jon and NoraLee Sedmak
Dasha Shenkman
Rita and Paul Skinner
Bruno Wang

Soul Mates
David and Corinne Abbott
Chris and Frances Bates
Ginny and Humphrey Battcock
Anthony and Karen Beare
Joanne Beckett
Lady Primrose Bell
Royce and Rotha Bell
Guy America and Dominique Bellec
The Bickertons
Adrian and Lisa Binks
James Brimlow
Beatrice Bondy
Katie Bradford
CJ and LM Braithwaite
Dr Neil and Sarah Brener
Clive and Helena Butler
Roger and Stephanie Carr
Georgina David
Roger and Alison De Haan
Scott M Delman
Annabel Duncan-Smith
Nicky Dunn
Jennifer and Jeff Eldredge

Sir Vernon and Lady Ellis
Don Ellwood and Sandra Johnigan
Ian and Margaret Frost
Jill and Jack Gerber
Sarah Hall
Katherine Hallgarten
Frances Hellman and Warren Breslau
Nik Holttum and Helen Brannigan
Jane Horrocks
Mike and Caroline Howes
Linden Ife
John and Gerry Kinder
Carol Lake
Anna Lane
Ken and Mimi Lamb
Jude Law
Victoria Leggett
Colette and Peter Levy
Chris and Jane Lucas
James and Sue Macmillan
Jill and Justin Manson
Sir Ian McKellen
Barbara Minto
Hala Mnaymneh
Miles Morland
Steven and Annie Murphy
Georgia Oetker
Rob and Lesley O'Rahilly
Heather and Julia Randall
Ron and Sue Sandler
Carol Sellars
Dr. Bhagat Sharma
Justin Shinebourne

Jenny Sheridan
Demola Soremekun
Nicola Stanhope
Sir Patrick Stewart
Jan and Michael Topham
Totally Theatre Productions
Katleen van Roost
Donna and Richard Vinter
Rob and Gillian Wallace
Edgar and Judith Wallner
Ian and Victoria Watson
Lucinda Watts
Bill and Anda Winters
Jill Hackel Zarzycki

And with thanks to all the Young Vic Friends and those donors who wish to remain anonymous.

Trust Supporters
95.8 Capital FM's Help a Capital Child
Amberstone Trust
The Andor Charitable Trust
The Austin & Hope Pilkington Trust
BBC Children in Need
Backstage Trust
Battersea Power Station Foundation
The Boris Karloff Foundation
Boshier Hinton Foundation

The Burford Cannell Charitable Trust

Chapman Charitable Trust

Charlotte Bonham-Carter Foundation

City Bridge Trust

Cleopatra Trust

Clifford Chance Foundation

The Clore Duffield Foundation

Cockayne – Grants for the Arts

The John S Cohen Foundation

The Co-operative Membership Community Fund

The Dr. Mortimer and Theresa Sackler Foundation

The D'Oyly Carte Charitable Trust

The Eranda Rothschild Foundation

The Ernest Cook Trust

The Evan Cornish Foundation

The Foyle Foundation

Garfield Weston Foundation

The Garrick Charitable Trust

Genesis Foundation

The Golden Bottle Trust

The Golsoncott Foundation

H&M Foundation

The Harold Hyam Wingate Foundation

The Jerwood Charitable Foundation

John Ellerman Foundation

The John Thaw Foundation

J. Paul Getty Jnr. Charitable Trust

The Kidron and Hall Family

The Leche Trust

The Limbourne Trust

The London Community Foundation

The Mackintosh Foundation

The Martin Bowley Charitable Trust

The Memery Crystal Charitable Trust

The Noël Coward Foundation

The Nomura Charitable Trust

Paul Hamlyn Foundation

David and Elaine Potter Foundation

The Portrack Charitable Trust

The Rayne Trust

Red Hill Trust

Richard Radcliffe Charitable Trust

Richenthal Foundation

Royal Victoria Hall Foundation

The Sackler Trust

Santander Foundation

United St Saviour's Charity

Unity Theatre Trust

Wellcome Trust

The Wolfson Foundation

National Theatre

The National Theatre makes world-class theatre that is entertaining, challenging and inspiring. And we make it for everyone.

We stage up to 30 productions at our South Bank home each year, ranging from reimagined classics – such as Greek tragedy and Shakespeare – to modern masterpieces and new work by contemporary writers and theatre-makers. The work we make strives to be as open, as diverse, as collaborative and as national as possible. Much of that new work is researched and developed at the New Work department: we are committed to nurturing innovative work from new writers, directors, creative artists and performers. Equally, we are committed to education, with a wide-ranging Learning programme for all ages in our Clore Learning Centre and in schools and communities across the UK.

The National's work is also seen on tour throughout the UK and internationally, and in collaborations and co-productions with regional theatres. Popular shows transfer to the West End and occasionally to Broadway. Through National Theatre Live, we broadcast live performances to cinemas around the world.

National Theatre: On Demand. In Schools makes acclaimed, curriculum-linked productions free to stream on demand in every primary and secondary school in the country. Online, the NT offers a rich variety of innovative digital content on every aspect of theatre.

We do all we can to keep ticket prices affordable and to reach a wide audience, and use our public funding to maintain artistic risk-taking, accessibility and diversity.

Chair of NT Board	**Sir Damon Buffini**
Deputy Chair	**Kate Mosse**
Director of the National Theatre	**Rufus Norris**
Executive Director	**Lisa Burger**

NT Board

Sir Damon Buffini (*Chair*), Kate Mosse (*Deputy Chair*),
Peter Bennett-Jones, Dame Ursula Brennan DCB, Sabine Chalmers,
Sir Lenny Henry, Vikki Heywood, Elizabeth Offord, Alan Rusbridger,
Tim Score, Clive Sherling, Simon Warshaw

NT Associates

Paul Arditti, Paule Constable, Dominic Cooke, Nadia Fall, Simon Godwin,
Kobna Holdbrook-Smith, Katrina Lindsay, Tom Morris, Lyndsey Turner

Senior Management

Deputy Artistic Director	**Ben Power**
Audiences and Marketing	**Alex Bayley**
Chief Operating Officer	**Liz Fosbury**
Commercial Operations	**Robyn Lines**
Communications	**Martin Prendergast**
Development	**Kathryn Marten**
Human Resources	**Tony Peers**
Information Technology	**Jon Cheyne**
Learning	**Alice King-Farlow**
NT Productions	**Kash Bennett**
Technical	**Jonathan Suffolk**

National Theatre
box office and information
+44 (0) 20 7452 3000

National Theatre, Upper Ground,
London SE1 9PX

nationaltheatre.org.uk

Registered Charity No: 224223
Registered as a company limited by guarantee in England: 749504

National Theatre Supporters

The Jungle **is supported by Glenn and Phyllida Earle
and Clive and Sally Sherling.**

Supporting the National Theatre

The National Theatre is a registered charity. It relies on support
from individuals, trusts and foundations and corporate organisations
to produce inspiring, challenging and entertaining theatre for everyone.

To find out more about how you can support the National Theatre, visit
nationaltheatre.org.uk/support-us

Supported using public funding by:

Travelex £15 Tickets
sponsored by

The National Theatre
in partnership with

Partner for Innovation

**Partner for
Learning**

Bank of America
Merrill Lynch

**Founding corporate
supporter for
Public Acts**

Bloomberg
Philanthropies

Partner for Connectivity

 ᢸᢍᢍᢍᢍ
CISCO

Outdoor Media Partner

Clear Channel
Where brands meet people

**Official
Airline**

▲ DELTA

Official Hotel Partner

EDWARDIAN
HOTELS
LONDON

International Hotel Partner

IHG° Rewards
Club

**Supporter for
new writing**

Cloud Services Partner

Pouring Partner

NYETIMBER
PRODUCT OF ENGLAND

**Partner for Lighting
and Energy**

PHILIPS
sense and simplicity

Sponsor of NT Live in the UK

The Royal National Theatre is a registered charity no.224223

Coming up at the National Theatre in 2018

OLIVIER THEATRE

Macbeth by William Shakespeare
From spring 2018
Twenty-five years after his last Shakespeare production, Rufus Norris directs
Rory Kinnear and Anne-Marie Duff in Shakespeare's darkest tragedy. Part of the
Travelex £15 Season.

Translations by Brian Friel
From May 2018
Ian Rickson directs a cast including Colin Morgan in Brian Friel's powerful account
of language and nationhood. Part of the Travelex £15 Season.

Exit the King by Eugène Ionesco, adapted by Patrick Marber
From July 2018
Patrick Marber directs his own adaptation of Ionesco's dark comedy. Cast includes
Rhys Ifans (King) and Indira Varma (Queen). Part of the Travelex £15 Season.

Pericles by William Shakespeare, adapted by Chris Bush
August 2018
Emily Lim directs a large community ensemble and small cast of professional
actors in the first Public Acts production.

Antony and Cleopatra by William Shakespeare
From September 2018
Simon Godwin follows the success of *Twelfth Night* with another Shakespeare
production in the Olivier. Ralph Fiennes and Sophie Okonedo play the lovers.

LYTTELTON THEATRE

Absolute Hell by Rodney Ackland
From April 2018
Joe Hill-Gibbins directs Ackland's plunge into post-war Soho, thirty years after
its rediscovery.

Julie by Polly Stenham
From June 2018
Carrie Cracknell directs this reimagining of Strindberg's *Miss Julie*, with a cast
which includes Vanessa Kirby. Part of the Travelex £15 Season.

The Lehman Trilogy by Stefano Massini, adapted by Ben Power
A co-production with Neal Street Productions
From July 2018
Sam Mendes directs the epic story of Lehman Brothers from its inception in 1844
to the financial crash 163 years later. Ben Power adapts Stefano Massini's play,
which has been a success across Europe.

I'm Not Running by David Hare

From autumn 2018

I'm Not Running, David Hare's eighteenth play at the National Theatre, is directed by Neil Armfield. It tells the story of two friends and their involvement, or lack of it, in British party politics.

DORFMAN THEATRE

John by Annie Baker

From early 2018

Following *The Flick* in 2016, Annie Baker returns to the Dorfman with her new play, *John*. James Macdonald directs the European premiere.

The Winter's Tale by William Shakespeare,
adapted by Justin Audibert and the company

February 2018

Justin Audibert directs an exciting new version of the Shakespeare play for primary school children. Shakespeare for younger audiences is supported by: The Ingram Trust, Archie Sherman Charitable Trust.

The Great Wave by Francis Turnly
A co-production with the Tricycle Theatre

From March 2018

Indhu Rubasingham, Artistic Director of the Tricycle Theatre, returns to the National Theatre to direct *The Great Wave* by Francis Turnly, who wrote it while on a Channel 4 playwriting bursary at the Kilburn theatre.

Nine Night by Natasha Gordon

From April 2018

Natasha Gordon's debut play is a funny and touching exploration of the rituals of family. *Nine Night* is directed by Roy Alexander Weise.

An Octoroon by Branden Jacobs-Jenkins
A co-production with Orange Tree Theatre

From June 2018

Ned Bennett's production of Branden Jacobs-Jenkins' satire was highly praised at Orange Tree Theatre.

Home, I'm Darling by Laura Wade
A co-production with Theatr Clwyd

From July 2018

Theatr Clwyd's Artistic Director Tamara Harvey directs Laura Wade's NT and Theatr Clwyd debut, a new comedy with cast including Katherine Parkinson. It will open at Theatr Clwyd in June before coming to the NT in July.

Good Chance builds temporary theatres of hope promoting freedom of expression, creativity and dignity for everyone. We believe in the unique ability of theatre and art to provide safety and comfort to people in desperate and challenging situations. We build theatres in areas where expression is stifled, where human rights are under threat and where communities are struggling to integrate. These theatres are safe spaces which give people the opportunity to express themselves, to engage in dialogue and debate, and to experience the enriching and transformative power of art.

Founded by two British playwrights, Joe Murphy and Joe Robertson, Good Chance established its first temporary theatre space, a large geodesic dome, in the heart of the refugee and migrant camp in Calais in September 2015. After seven months in Calais, the theatre travelled to London's Southbank Centre for for a vibrant nine-day arts festival led by refugees in July 2016. In early 2017, Good Chance began working in Paris, starting with a five-week residence at La Station, Gare de Mines, in collaboration with Collectif MU and Emmaüs Solidarité. From here, the Good Chance dome travelled to the gardens of Théâtre de la Ville for the duration of the Chantiers d'Europe Festival. In January 2018 Good Chance will return to Paris at the invitation of the Mayor of Paris and Emmaüs Solidarité to run the theatre alongside the main migrant welcome centre in the north of the city.

Good Chance is an Associate Company of the Young Vic Theatre and recipient of the Evening Standard Editor's Award (2016), an Empty Space Peter Brook Award (2016), and was nominated in 2016 for the Index on Censorship Freedom of Expression Award and The Stage International Award.

'I really thank the people who organise this great theatre. And we will know many things by it. For example, show different cultures, different people with different mind and language as well. So it doesn't matter how you look like, just be the best version of yourself.

Just come to the theatre. Even you will get knowledge from it.

You read story from ancient time up to now and sing a song. Wisdom. Really it's great idea to come to the theatre to know more about it.

Follow your ideas. Don't follow the other people ideas. Your mind is the best mind. And don't care what they're saying. Once again, thanks for the people who organised – God bless you.'

Alsadig from Sudan, fifteen years old,
a regular visitor to Good Chance Calais

'A varied programme of music, drama, poetry, movement and debate, for and by the inhabitants of the camp, occupies the Good Chance theatre six days a week. All by itself it proclaims that life without culture is nothing but biology in survival mode. That was the lesson we brought home.'

Sir Tom Stoppard, *Sunday Times*

Artistic Directors	**Joe Murphy**
	and **Joe Robertson**
Executive Director	**Naomi Webb**
International Executive Producer	**Claire Béjanin**
Press and PR Manager	**Jenn Reynolds**
Artistic Associate	**Amy Reade**
Administrative Assistant	**Lydia Paulett**
Accountants	**Inda Bunyan**
	and **Keith Cunningham**

Board of Trustees
Stephen Daldry (Chair), Sonia Friedman, Natalia Kaliada, David Lan

Good Chance Supporters

For their support of *The Jungle* we would like to thank:

The KT Wong Foundation, Karen Bastick-Styles and the students and staff at Greenside School and The Elliot Foundation, Giulio Piscitelli, Jeff Culpepper and Susan Witherow and all the individuals who participated in the development of the production: Majid Adin, Jude Akuwudike, Rob Callender, Mike Cunningham, Andy De La Tour, Sharief Dorani, Jack Ellis, Amir El-Masry, Yolli Fuller, Annie Gavrilescu, Sue Gladys Harvey, Baraa Halabieh, Richard Hansell, Faisal Harbi, Ben Harrison, Paul Hilton, David Lan, Amra Mallassi, Adam Mohammedean Khamees, Hamed Moradi, Yasin Moradi, Charles Mnene, Conor Neaves, Con O'Neill, Sophie Stanton, Alex Sutton, Bernie Whittle and everyone at the National Theatre New Work Department.

For their time, wisdom and support since we first built our theatre in Calais in 2015 we would like to thank:

Cyril Cadars, Claire Calligaro, Henry Culpepper, Jeff Culpepper, Tory Davidson, Lucy Davies, Fenella Dawnay, Dominique Delport, Elyse Dodgson, Mike Downey, Sean Egan, Vicky Featherstone, Eric Fellner, Annie Gavrilescu, Alan Gartland, Patrick Glackin, Laura Griffiths, Baraa Halabieh, Andy Harries, Elizabeth Kesses, David Lan, Maddy Moore, Patricia Moyersoen, Charles Mnene, Carey Mulligan, Sarah Murray, Anna Murphy, Rufus Norris, Joanna Ostrom, Jemma Read, Ian Rickson, Kate Robertson, Tracey Seaward, Mike Shepherd, Kirstin Shirling, Suzanne Smalley, Chris Sonnex, Juliet Stevenson, Vanessa Stone, Mark Tildesley, Claire Verlet, Dagmar Walz, Bruno Wang, Emily Webb, Mat Whitecross, Susan Witherow, Lena Zimmer, Zoukak and everyone who has volunteered with us in the UK, France and across the world.

And we extend an enormous thank you to:

to all the individuals and organisations whose donations and grants have made it possible for us to build a theatre in Calais and continue Good Chance's work across the world for more than two years. Without you none of this would have been possible.

Good Chance relies on donations and grants and if you would like to support the continued work of the company both in the UK and internationally, we would love to hear from you on:

hello@goodchance.org.uk / +44 (0)20 7922 2994

c/o Young Vic, 66 The Cut, London, SE1 8LZ

www.goodchance.org.uk

 GoodChanceTheatre

 @goodchancecal

 goodchancetheatre

Registered charity number 1166833

Help Refugees

From their beginnings as a young grassroots collective, Help Refugees is now the leading UK NGO in a new movement of humanitarian aid. Acting where government and other non-governmental bodies are unable to, they work to fill the gaps in services for those displaced by war in Europe and beyond.

www.helprefugees.org

Citizens UK

The home of community organising in the UK, Citizens UK organises communities to act together for power, social justice and common good, so that members can hold politicians and decision makers to account on the issues that matter to them.

www.citizensuk.org

Safe Passage

Safe Passage exists to help unaccompanied child refugees and vulnerable adults find safe, legal routes to sanctuary, supporting them in their first steps to rebuilding their lives in the UK.

www.safepassage.org.uk

The Elliot Foundation

The Elliot Foundation is a multi-academy trust that aims to build self-improving, self-sustaining clusters of top primary academies, supporting them to give students a brighter future. At Greenside School students work as a Film Factory based on a unique experiential learning model striving to break boundaries and inspire students through film and the arts. Greenside students are challenged to be independent thinkers, to be World Ready and Test Ready and to contribute to the world as international citizens. The Elliot Foundation and Greenside School are proud to support *The Jungle*.

www.elliotfoundation.co.uk / www.greensideschool.org

Good Chance Theatre is supported by the KT Wong Foundation

PRINCIPAL PRODUCTION SUPPORTER, GOOD CHANCE THEATRE

Established in 2007, The KT Wong Foundation has been a catalyst for innovative artistic practice and cross-cultural dialogue in opera, theatre and across the arts.

The Jungle is a play which vividly asserts the value of human connection and dignity through the stories of migration, hardship and hope. The KT Wong Foundation is proud to act as Principal Production Supporter for Good Chance Theatre.

Projects in 2017 include a critically lauded new production of the opera *Greek* by Mark-Anthony Turnage, chosen to open the Edinburgh International Festival, and a music commission by composer Neo Muyanga to accompany a new film by artist Mohau Modisakeng, South Africa's co-representative at the 57th Venice Biennale.

In its second decade, the Foundation is more intent than ever on connecting cultures through creativity and artistic ambition. In the words of Lady Davies, 'The arts are a vital pathway for us in search of a more nuanced understanding of what brings us together, and keeps us apart, in the modern world.'

www.ktwong.org

The Jungle

Joe Murphy grew up in Leeds and Joe Robertson grew up in Hull. They began writing plays together at university in 2011. Their short plays include *Fairway Manor* (Burton Taylor Studio, Oxford Playhouse), *Ten Bits on Boondoggling* and *Paper Play* (Edinburgh Fringe) and *Maria Popova* (Greater Manchester tram network). In 2015, they established Good Chance Theatre in the 'Jungle' refugee and migrant camp in Calais, a space of expression where theatre, art, dance and music could be made. They lived there for seven months until the eviction of the southern half of the camp. In 2016, Good Chance built its original Calais theatre in view of the UK Parliament for *Encampment*, a major festival at the Southbank Centre in London, with a programme of 110 artists from around the world, run by former residents of the camp. Good Chance then began working in Paris with theatres, humanitarian organisations and local communities to create new spaces of expression, welcome and introductions. In January 2018, two new temporary theatres of hope are planned to open in the north of Paris. *The Jungle* is Joe and Joe's first full-length play.

JOE MURPHY
and
JOE ROBERTSON

The Jungle

FABER & FABER

First published in 2017
by Faber and Faber Limited
74–77 Great Russell Street
London WC1B 3DA

Typeset by Country Setting, Kingsdown, Kent CT14 8ES
Printed in England by CPI Group (UK) Ltd, Croydon CR0 4YY

All rights reserved

Copyright © Joe Murphy and Joe Robertson. 2017

Joe Murphy and Joe Robertson are hereby identified
as authors of this work in accordance with Section 77
of the Copyright, Designs and Patents Act 1988

All rights whatsoever in this play are strictly reserved and
application for performance etc. should be made in writing,
before rehearsals begin, to Judy Daish Associates Ltd,
2 St Charles Place, London W10 6EG. No performance
may be given unless a licence has first been obtained

*This book is sold subject to the condition that it shall not,
by way of trade or otherwise, be lent, resold, hired out or otherwise
circulated without the publisher's prior consent in any form
of binding or cover other than that in which it is published
and without a similar condition including this condition
being imposed on the subsequent purchaser*

A CIP record for this book is available from the British Library

ISBN 978–0–571–34624–0

FSC
www.fsc.org
MIX
Paper from
responsible sources
FSC® C013604

2 4 6 8 10 9 7 5 3

For Sonia and Stephen

The Jungle, a co-production between Young Vic and the National Theatre with Good Chance Theatre, commissioned by the National Theatre, opened at the Young Vic on 7 December 2017. The cast, in alphabetical order, was as follows:

Henri/Yasin Raphael Acloque
Amal Aliya Ali, Alyssa Denise D'Souza
Norullah Mohammad Amiri
Muzamil Elham Ehsas
Boxer Trevor Fox
Omid Moein Ghobsheh
Derek Michael Gould
Safi Ammar Haj Ahmad
Mohammed Ansu Kabia
Yohannes Bruk Kumelay
Sam Alex Lawther
Paula Jo McInnes
Okot John Pfumojena
Beth Rachel Redford
Ali Rachid Sabitri
Omar Mohamed Sarrar
Salar Ben Turner
Helene Nahel Tzegai

Direction Stephen Daldry and Justin Martin
Design Miriam Buether
Costume Catherine Kodicek
Light Jon Clark
Sound Paul Arditti
Composer and Musical Direction John Pfumojena
Video Tristan Shepherd

Casting Julia Horan, CDG
Fights Terry King
Voice Jeannette Nelson
Creative Consultant Amy Reade
Assistant Director Nicole Charles
Design Assistant Joana Dias
Video Producer Tamara Moore
Archive Research Belinda Harris

Characters

Ali
thirties, Kurdistan

Beth
eighteen, UK

Boxer
forties, UK

CRS Officer
France

Derek
fifties, UK

Helene
twenty-eight, Eritrea

Henri
twenties, France

Little Amal
six, Syria

Maz
twenty, Afghanistan

Mohammed
thirty-five, Sudan

Norullah
fifteen, Afghanistan

Okot
seventeen, Sudan

Omar
twenty-five, Sudan

Omid
twenty-one, Iran

Paula
fifties, UK

Safi
thirty-five, Syria

Salar
thirty-two, Afghanistan

Sam
eighteen, UK

Yasin
twenty-four, Iraq

Yohannes
twenty-one, Ethiopia

THE JUNGLE

'The desperate desire of everyone is that this
is a temporary stop. A brief, cold and trying moment.
But despite the best intentions, the Jungle is beginning
to become a place, with churches and theatres and art
and restaurants. It is germinating into that collective
home. But then, isn't this how all places once began?
With refugees stopping at a river, a beach, a crossroads,
and saying, we'll just pause here for a bit. Put on the
kettle, kill a chicken.'

A.A. Gill

*This version of the text went to press
while rehearsals were still in progress, and may
differ slightly from the play as performed.*

ONE
THE JUDGEMENT

February 2016.

An emergency meeting of residents and volunteers inside a makeshift Afghan restaurant in the Jungle refugee and migrant camp in Calais, France.

It is late at night, freezing cold. The restaurant is restless and busy. More and more people congregate, meeting, embracing, exchanging. People wait, smoke, talk, sip sweet milky chai. Hot naan bake in an oven and are passed around.

Paula is recording the names and details of residents. Little Amal, a young girl, is always by her side.

Everyone is dirty, exhausted, wide-eyed on energy drinks, emotional, frightened, cold. Deep, rattling coughs punctuate the noise of talk in many languages and multiple generators growling all around.

Everything happens quickly in the Jungle, all at once, everyone on top of each other and always present.

Derek addresses the room.

Derek Right. Can I have everyone's attention, please? I know there have been a lot of rumours going around. People are frightened. I'm going to explain as clearly as I can the facts as we know them. Can you translate that, please?

Mohammed Arabic. (*Translates.*)

Salar Pashto. (*Translates.*)

Helene Tigrinya. (*Translates.*)

Ali Kurdish. (*Translates.*)

Paula Salar, I need your information.

Salar Salar Malikzai. Thirty-two. Afghanistan. Eleven months.

Derek Another eviction notice was posted this morning. It gives police the authority to clear all the southern half of the Jungle. That includes the school, the mosques, the churches. Most of the shops . . .

Salar My restaurant?

Derek Yes, it includes the restaurants. Translators.

Translations.

Paula Mohammed.

Mohammed Mohammed Abboud. Thirty-five. Sudan. Eleven months.

Derek The Judge has said it must be an expulsion –

Sam An *expulsion humanitaire* –

Derek A soft eviction, which means no bulldozers. We've heard that the police –

Beth enters.

Beth Sorry, everyone. Sorry, Derek. A boy has gone missing.

Derek Beth –

Beth Norullah, he's fifteen, from Afghanistan. You all know him.

Derek Beth, not now –

Beth If anyone sees him, tell me, tell Paula, tell Salar.

She exits.

Derek We've heard that maybe the police will start doing something tomorrow. So it's likely, if that happens, they will just be asking people to leave.

Paula Helene.

Helene Helene Gebrekidane. Twenty-eight. Eritrea. Eleven months.

Mohammed How can this be legal? They cannot evict us in the middle of winter!

Derek They can't. That's why we're mounting an appeal, Sam.

Salar Oh, here he is.

Sam The notice is legal because the government has said it will rehouse everyone, in accommodation centres around France.

Salar Your friends?

Derek Salar, please.

Salar He is a collaborator.

Sam Which would be fine, but they are only providing fifteen hundred spaces.

Helene This is joke!

Sam Obviously, it's completely wrong.

Salar How can we trust a word you say?

Derek Salar –

Salar No, no, no, this boy is a liar!

Derek Calm, please –

Sam Unless we can prove, prove to the courts there are many, many more people –

Salar No more evictions. That's what you said!

Sam And clearly they've fucked us.

Salar goes for Sam. He is held back.

Paula The police are lining up out there and we're fighting each other!

Derek Sam, let's go.

Derek pulls Sam away.

Paula We are conducting a census. A record of every man, woman and child living in the Jungle today. Age. Country. Time you've been here. I need this from everyone.

Omar (*Arabic*) What does she want our information for? She's police!

Mohammed The census is not for France asylum. Not for deporting. Trust the lady.

Paula Thank you, Mohammed. This is how we are going to fight. Legally. Peacefully. Omar.

Omar Omar Sarrah. Twenty-five. Sudan. Seven months.

Beth enters.

Beth Paula, have you seen him?

Paula No.

Beth His name must be on here.

Paula I haven't seen him.

Beth Norullah Abdul!

Paula Beth –

Beth Where the hell is he?

She exits.

Paula Omid.

Omid Omid Torkan. Twenty-one. Iran. Four months.

Derek hands out forms.

Derek If you run a business, fill out a form. What you do. How many people you serve. Cafés, shops, restaurants, Salar. Hairdressers, mosques, churches . . .

Paula's phone rings.

Sam Volunteers, Derek.

Derek Volunteers, if you run a kitchen, distribution point, women and children's centre, anything. Fill it in.

Paula (*ending the call*) Fuck's sake. Boxer, are you sober?

Boxer All things considered.

Paula Can I trust you with something?

Boxer What do I say to that?

Paula Yes, Paula. You can.

Boxer Yes, Paula. Course you bloody can.

Paula Look after Amal. (*To Amal.*) I'll be back soon, love. Stay with Uncle Boxer.

Boxer Howay, pet.

Paula Don't let her out of your sight. (*Handing the census to Derek.*) Derek, finish this off. A boy's been killed on the motorway.

Derek I heard.

Salar Who?

Paula I'm going to identify the body.

She leaves.
Mohammed is filling in a form for Salar.

Mohammed Salar, how many people come here?

Salar Everyone.

Mohammed What service do you provide?

Salar Have you tasted my rice and beans?

Mohammed Why is your restaurant vital to life in the Jungle?

Salar (*taking a framed review off the wall*) Give them that.

Mohammed We need to do this, Salar.

Salar Jungle finished. We have said it for months. Now it's true.

Henri (*to Sam*) Let's speak honestly. As friends. There isn't any more you can do here. I know you built houses. I know you helped. Now they will be destroyed and that's difficult for you, I understand.

Sam No more evictions. You promised me.

Henri Come on, you can't have thought it would last for ever. Go home and rest. Be with your family. And then do something great with your life.

Sam The Judge will rule in our favour.

Henri Here is the contact of my successor.

Sam You're leaving?

Henri For Paris. I would be very sad if our relationship were to end this way.

Sam The whole camp hates me. They're calling me a collaborator. Would this be happening if I hadn't helped you?

Henri A piece of advice. Don't stay here. It isn't safe.

Derek addresses the room.

Derek The census is complete! We have the results! Translators? 5,497 people live in the Jungle. 3,455 in the eviction zone. 445 of those are children. 305

unaccompanied. Now we know who we are. This eviction is illegal.

Cheers, as Paula enters.

Paula Please, please, give me good news.

Derek Court's adjourned.

Sam Their figures are wrong. We have a case.

Derek Was it him?

Paula Yes.

Derek Are you sure?

They look to Salar.

Paula Salar. The boy on the motorway. It was Norullah.

Pause.

I'm sorry.

He leaves.

Mohammed Ali, Omar, Omid.

They leave, as Beth enters.

Beth What's going on?

Sam There was a death on the motorway this morning.

Beth I heard.

Sam A young boy.

Beth Right . . .

Sam An Afghan.

Beth What are you saying?

Sam You know what I'm saying.

Beth You're wrong.

Sam Paula identified the body.

Beth Don't call it that.

Paula They're burying him in the cemetery. Angel's corner.

Beth How can they bury him in the mud in Calais?

Derek The Judge is giving her verdict. Sam.

He passes his phone to Sam, who translates from French.

Sam She has considered the case carefully . . . she recognises that the *bidonville* represents a serious risk to public safety and decency . . .

Boxer Bidon – what?

Derek Slum.

Sam She . . . also recognises the significant infrastructure within the *bidonville* –

Boxer That's a slum, that is.

Sam – *les lieux de vie*, the places of life . . . she recognises a difference between the official population figures and those presented by organisations working within the *bidonville* . . .

Derek We won!

Sam However . . .

Derek However?

Sam She . . . has not been convinced that this evidence is sufficient to change her first verdict . . . consequently . . . she upholds the notice and gives legal authorisation for the eviction to begin.

Numbed silence.

Derek No . . .

Boxer Bugger that.

Paula What more do they fucking want?

The body of a boy is carried on, shrouded in white, raised into the air, bathed in light, then buried. The following Surah is spoken in Arabic.

Omar In the name of Allah, Most Gracious, Ever Merciful. All types of perfect praise belong to Allah alone, the Lord of all the worlds, Most Gracious, Ever Merciful, Master of the Day of Judgement. Thee alone do we worship and Thee alone do we implore for help . . .

Guide us along the straight path – the path of those on whom Thou hast bestowed Thy favours, those who have not incurred Thy displeasure, and those who have not gone astray.

Okot enters slowly.

Beth Okot, what are you doing here?

Okot (*Arabic*) Who is it?

Beth Okot!

Ali (*Arabic*) What the fuck are you doing here? (*English.*) You should be in Dunkirk.

Beth Dunkirk? You told me he was in the UK.

Ali You know nothing about this.

Beth We had an agreement, you promised to keep him safe.

Ali Omid!

He calls someone on his phone.

Okot This is not good man. This is bad man.

Ali Omid, grab him . . .

Beth Okot, come here.

Okot No good man here. I'm sorry, Beth. I'm so sorry I make problem. Sorry I make him dead. Sorry for everything.

He runs.

Beth Okot!

Beth is restrained by Paula.

Paula What have you done?

Mohammed Get out of here, Ali. Go!

Ali leaves.

Salar Oh! Allah, make him, this child, our means of preservation, and make him a source of reward and treasure for us, and make him a pleader for us, and one whose pleading is accepted.

Mohammed You were close to him.

Salar Like my son.

Mohammed Did he have parents?

Salar His mother in Kabul. He phoned her every week, told her he was in UK. In London, with his friends. He was in a house. A family had taken him in. He had made photographs in front of Big Ben. He was starting at a school. He was learning English.

Paula And he was. Here.

Salar Yes. He told her he was happy. I have to tell her he didn't even make it out of France.

Derek This isn't your fault.

Salar I kept him here.

Paula (*to a TV camera*) Four hundred and fifty kids. Three hundred alone. That's more than at my daughter's school. Kids riding bikes through mud. Surviving winter in tents. Wind off the sea. Cold. Angel's corner. That's the muddy patch at the edge of a graveyard full of little wooden crosses.

Fucking dump. Fucking hell on earth. Built some cardboard boxes and painted pictures for a bit of fucking hope. Yeah, knock it down. Knock it down and never let it happen again. But not like this. Not when they have nowhere to go. Kids will disappear, mark my word. Hundreds of them. They'll run, or be taken, we'll never see them again. And you'll be the ones asking what happened. Mark my word.

She leaves.

Boxer looks around. Only he and Amal are left in the restaurant.

Boxer (*to Amal as he dresses her in warm clothes*) Y'alright, pet. Has anyone ever told you about England? Because it's a land full of green fields and great, long rivers. Tiny island out on its own. And because it's so small, everyone has to be kind. They have to get on and make things work. There's parks with slides, big swings. Beautiful, old schools –

Amal School.

Boxer Ay, that's right. Teachers who love you. And anywhere you go, any time of day, you're always welcome. And don't let anyone tell you otherwise.

Now, it's all getting a bit messy here, so you're going to come with me. Arms up. This jumper belongs to a very special girl. She's called Lottie. You'll meet her soon. She's going to be your big sister.

We're going to go for a little drive now, and you have to be nice and quiet. It's like hide and seek. And I promise you. You'll forget all about this place.

If there's one thing I know, I've been a shit dad. All that's going to change.

Boxer and Amal exit.

Derek (*to the room, as he hands out scarves*) When the police arrive they will arrive with orders. They will use tear gas, which is banned by the Geneva Convention for use in warfare, but there are no laws against it here. Tear gas is a nerve agent. It acts by irritating mucus membranes in the eyes, nose, mouth and lungs. When they shoot, you need to cover your face. If you are exposed, use milk or Coke to wash it off, not water. Do not wear gas masks, the police consider them weapons. They themselves will be heavily armed and wearing body armour. This dehumanises them. But they are human beings like us. It is our job to re-humanise the situation. They cannot be violent if they see that you are a person, a human being like them.

Mohammed runs in.

Mohammed They are here! They are gassing! They have bulldozers!

Derek They can't. The Judge said a soft eviction.

Members of the Compagnies Républicaines de Sécurité (CRS) shoot tear gas into the restaurant.

Paula Amal! Amal!

Derek It can't end like this!

Paula Where the fuck is Boxer?

Mohammed It's time, my friend. To the port.

A huge explosion outside. Salar smiles.

Salar No. We resist.

He stands on a table, raises a sign which reads:

WE ARE SEARCHING FOR FREEDOM IN EUROPE
BUT WE FIND NONE

24

Sam Beth, come on!

Beth I can't.

Sam We have to go now!

A CRS Officer enters in full riot gear, stares at them both.

CRS Officer *Bouges-toi!*

Beth I won't move.

CRS Officer Don't understand you, girl.

Beth I'm not leaving him here. I can't leave, I'll never leave.

CRS Officer You are in France, you speak French!

Beth stands and faces him.

Beth Look at yourself! This is not France!

The Officer aims a pepper spray canister into her eyes. Safi walks calmly into the pandemonium.

Safi Stop.

TWO
THE BIRTH

In peace and quiet, he addresses everyone.

Safi They warned us in Libya. The smugglers. They advised us about safe passage. How to stay hidden, avoid arrest. And one thing they say to me, again and again, I remember . . .

'Beware the French. They have absolutely no manners.'

My name is Safi Al-Hussain, thirty-five years young. Former student of English literature and languages in my home town, Aleppo, so I know a little bit about telling stories.

Another quotation for you. 'If you open me up when I am dead, you will find Calais engraved upon my heart.'

One of your queens said that. Is it true for you? Maybe because your armies fought over Calais for so many centuries, which is bizarre to me – have you ever been there?! Or maybe, if you like history, it is because you know Julius Caesar invaded you from Calais in 54 BC. Or maybe the other BC? *Booze cruise.*

Open me up. You'll find it there, engraved upon my heart. Like many before me, I lived there to get here. And it takes pain to live side by side. If you are born in the same country as another person this is true. If you are born in a different country, a different continent, even more. Some people will tell you it is easy, but you mustn't trust them. These are difficult things, my friends. I do not pretend we did not make mistakes.

And many more will be made in the telling of this story, I am sure.

March 2015 is the date of birth.

Salar and Mohammed meet. They are cleaner, more awake, looking years younger.

Mohammed What a dump.

Safi Mohammed Abboud. From Darfur.

Mohammed This is the worst place in Europe.

Salar Tonight we will be free.

Mohammed If we live that long.

Salar They said this land is ours to use. We can build here!

Safi Salar Malikzai. From Karz, near Kandahar.

More people enter, carrying bags, tents and sleeping bags.

Mohammed Let's count the things that kill us. Chemicals, snakes, the filthy land, all rubbish –

Salar Is better than bombs, Mohammed.

Mohammed Cold, wind, rain –

Salar Terrorists, the Taliban –

Mohammed The CRS –

Salar Drought, famine –

Mohammed Each other?

Salar We are safer than at any time in our lives.

Mohammed There are tensions between our people. Before, we lived in separate places. Now, we must live together.

Salar So we live apart.

Mohammed There isn't space to live apart.

Salar Look around. It's already done.

They divide the land.

Ali This is Kurdistan.

Yasin Here is Iraq.

Omid This Iran.

Helene Eritrea.

Safi Syria.

Salar Sudan?

Mohammed If this is going to work, you and I must stand together.

Salar We will, my friend. We will.

Mohammed Sudan.

Salar And this is Afghanistan.

An Afghan flag is raised as Norullah and Maz sing the national anthem. Salar translates.

This land is Afghanistan, the pride of every Afghan!
The land of peace, the land of the sword – its sons
    are all brave!
This is the country of every tribe!

Safi We were forced from many places into one, and this place we called:

Salar Zhangal!

A drumbeat begins.

Safi A Pashto word. In its great wisdom, France made Zhangal only a short walk to the ferry port. Everyone tries. You know this word, a good word, all languages understand. Try is the reason we are here. Try for train. Try for boat. The first nights, it is like the sea is in two parts and we walk to UK on a simple path. So many try, so many succeed!

People try to cross the border.
    Little Amal darts around, person to person.

All Yayayayayayayayayaya!

Safi The sound we make when someone arrives safe. This is good chance. Good chance is the dream.

Norullah No chance!

Okot Police at port!

Safi So we go for the trains.

Norullah No chance!

Okot Police at train!

Safi So we go back for the port!

Norullah Dugar! Dugar! Dugar!

Safi Dugar is a miracle. Dugar means traffic jam. When lorries begin to slow and horns are loud, we see our dreams may happen.

All Yayayayayayayayayaya!

Safi We call it the game! We are young men. Strong, brave. We climb fences, jump lorries, escape police. And, if I can say, it is *fun*. Yes, sometimes they catch us. But French police are strange. They let you go every time. To try and try again! Go back to Zhangal –

All No chance!

Sunrise.

Safi This was night, and in the day we built. Everywhere, the sound of saws, hammers, work. In the absence of any help from the French state, we did it ourselves.

Henri enters in hi-vis, with protection.

Henri (*French*) No, no. We built a centre. Le Centre de Jules Ferry. With sleeping places for women and children. Showers.

People object to his speaking in French.

Safi My friend, no one here speaks French.

Henri We built a compound for women and children. There are sleeping places. Showers. Funded by the generosity of the French state. And we will give one meal a day.

Safi For how many people? There are hundreds arriving every day.

Henri exits.

For the marathons we run each night, one meal is nothing. It is hungry work, trying for your country.

Mohammed lights a fire.

Sudanese sits all day with three logs of burning wood. He blows, cares for it.

Mohammed Tomato, tuna fish, big bread!

Salar fires up a large gas cylinder.

Safi Afghan cooks stewed meat.

Salar Tender. Fluffy rice with sultanas. Red bean sauce. Chicken liver.

Safi People meet and laugh and eat together. Share stories of great journeys, with excitement like I have never heard.

The call to prayer sounds.

This was five times a day at home. Now it is from mosques in Zhangal. It means, 'Come to pray. Come to *success.*' At home they were fighting. In Zhangal they were praying, Sunni and Shia together.

Helene sings 'Lord Have Mercy'.

Christians, too. The church of St Michael, protector and leader of army of God. With a makeshift steeple, six metres high. Images of the Virgin and Winnie the Pooh. The church of your imagination.

Helene Everyone is welcome to bask in the glory of the Lord!

Safi Beautiful words.

Helene God gave me them to help refugees.

Everyone joins in the song.

Safi You know this song? Maybe you learnt it in school. 'Lord Have Mercy'. In Tigrinya.

Yasin (*to Ali, in Arabic*) Can you get me across the border?

Ali What?

Safi Speak English.

Yasin I'm so cold. France police hit me. No food. Sleeping bag wet.

Ali It is not a good place.

Yasin You can help me?

Ali What kind of help are you looking for?

Yasin You know.

Everyone looks at Ali.

Ali You want help too, my friends?

Ali hands them pieces of paper with his number on.

Call me.

Safi More people means more opportunity.

He is nearly knocked over by a young boy on a bike overfilled with Lidl bags.

Safi You OK, my friend?

Norullah Fucking dick!

Safi Where's all this from?

Norullah Lidl.

Safi Lidl. Another Pashto word?

Norullah Fucking shop.

Safi This is a lot of food. Is it all for you?

Norullah I sell.

Safi And people buy it?

Norullah If I sell, people buy.

Salar Bambino! Quick!

Safi Clever boy.

Norullah runs to Salar, who sends him back to retrieve more bags.

Salar If we do this, we do it properly. You understand?

Norullah I'm not bambino.

Salar Norullah, my man. My restaurant man.

*They begin to build a restaurant.
Okot enters and rifles through Norullah's bags.*

Safi A restaurant. Mosques, churches, shops. And people from many countries for the first time living together in peace . . .

Norullah notices Okot.

Norullah What the fuck, fucking black man, fucking thief!

Okot I was only looking! Crazy fucking Afghan.

Norullah All you fucking black man same. Big problem!

Mohammed and Salar separate them. After consulting Okot and Norullah, they meet where the boys were. It could be a stand-off, but the situation settles.

Safi Problem. Another word. (*To the group.*) More people means more problems.

Mohammed The Galloo squat has been evicted. Three hundred people are waiting under the bridge.

Salar What are they waiting for?

Mohammed There aren't enough tents!

Helene People are sleeping in my church.

Salar After good chance tonight, there will be tents tomorrow.

Mohammed And then more people again.

Safi Eight thousand landed on Lesvos yesterday.

Salar How do you know this?

Safi The Facebook and WhatsApp groups say it. The same number crossed to Macedonia over the weekend. The Balkans route is full.

Salar Always on your phone.

Mohammed Phone is how we got here.

Helene When I crossed it was three or four boats in the week.

Salar They go to Germany.

Ali Not all. Many are coming here.

Salar Why is he in my restaurant?

Safi He speaks for the Kurdish people. Mohammed, Sudan. Helene, Eritrea. And I speak for Syria.

Salar Speak for?

Ali Doesn't look like a restaurant to me.

Salar It's not finished.

Ali I'll make sure I come back when it is.

Salar No smugglers allowed.

Ali You can afford to turn away business?

Salar I made it this far without you. I think I will manage.

Mohammed Gentlemen. We've come here to talk about violence. Not make more. We have a duty.

Salar Duty to who?

Mohammed Our people.

Salar Our *people*?

Mohammed These boys, Salar.

Salar To make the sun shine? To make the rain stop? To open the border?

Safi To work together.

Salar What problems?

Helene Toilets.

Salar Tell your *people* to shit properly.

Ali points to Maz, who is pissing nearby. Salar shouts at him and he runs off.

Helene It is difficult with so much infection.

Safi Another problem.

Salar So they should wash properly!

Helene Police violence.

Salar It is their job. It's the same everywhere.

Mohammed Fighting. Our young boys, Salar. It is not long before someone is killed.

Salar The Sudanese are thieves.

Mohammed Afghans are racist.

Salar If a black man steals can we not say?

Helene Always, always problem!

Safi This is what I'm talking about. We need to act before it gets out of control.

Salar How?

Safi We ask our Imams to talk about peace in their khutbas tomorrow.

Salar Fine.

Safi And we should walk through the camp together. Speak to everyone. Hand in hand.

Salar We needed a meeting to decide this?

Safi Yes.

Salar Do you speak for Syria or the whole camp? I am not an elder.

Mohammed But you are respected. Afghanistan is one of the largest communities –

Salar The largest.

Safi Without you there is no hope, Salar.

Mohammed We can meet here in your restaurant, when it's finished?

Ali It will be good for business.

Safi What do you think?

Pause.

Salar (*Pashto*) Norullah, come here. Shake his hand.

Norullah (*Pashto*) I'm not touching him.

Salar (*Pashto*) You do what I say.

Norullah steps towards Okot.

Mohammed (*to Okot, Arabic*) Go to him. Shake his hand.

They shake hands.

Salar No more fighting. We are hated by enough people. We do not hate each other.

Mohammed Thank you, Salar.

Safi It is August. We have been in Zhangal five months. More and more people arrive, making journeys across the terrible sea. Walking through Europe, like we did, with our phones, to safety. To our dreams. Yes, Zhangal is unclean. Yes, it smells. Yes, nowhere to shit. Sometimes good chance, sometimes no chance. Yes, little food, water, space, tents, clothes. Yes, you see children play in European mud.

Residents from many nationalities start to arrive at Salar's restaurant.

But more. More hope than you have seen in all lifetimes. More people of heart and song than you have ever heard. When you do not have enough of anything, you make from nothing.

Salar My restaurant is open!

Norullah My restaurant!

Salar The Afghan Flag. A traditional Afghan restaurant, serving traditional Afghan food.

Afghan music and dance commences.

Safi Great is the hope that makes man cross border.

All Yayayayayayayayayayaya!

A celebration, driven by tiredness and squalor. A collision of music and dance from many nationalities, as Salar, supported by workers, serves the first meal.
Into this walks Beth. She is holding her phone, which displays the photograph of Alan Kurdi.
The restaurant falls silent.

Safi Then, in September, everything changed.

Beth A photograph of a boy. A little boy. Washed up on a beach.

Safi Alan. Alan Kurdi. From Kobani in northern Syria. Please, come in. Would you like –

Norullah goes to her, stuffs fresh naan into her hands.

Norullah Best bread in France!

Beth Thank you!

Norullah You are UK. You have good seat.

Beth I don't need –

Norullah Sit. I am Norullah.

Beth Hello, Norullah. I'm Beth.

Norullah Miss Beth. I am one-five.

Beth Fifteen. I am one-eight.

Norullah But I am not bambino. I am restaurant man.

Beth It's a beautiful restaurant.

Norullah English no good. Kabul.

Beth Afghanistan?

Norullah You know?!

Beth I haven't been, but –

Norullah Afghanistan best country in world. Except one. You know!

Beth Do I?

He bursts out laughing.

Norullah You stay. I bring tea.

He runs to the kitchen.

Safi We spend months trying to get to UK. And in September, UK came here.

The music returns and slowly builds as each volunteer arrives.
Paula enters.

Paula I've got a thousand tents in the back of a truck. Anyone? Who the fuck's in charge here?

Little Amal runs towards Paula.

Hello, love. She's a baby. (*To Safi.*) Where's her mum and dad?

Safi Not here.

Paula Go and get them. She shouldn't be running around the mud on her own.

Safi I mean they're not in France.

Paula This isn't France, it's a fucking joke. Where's the UN?

Safi They have to be invited.

Paula Save the Children?

Safi Haven't seen them.

Paula Fucking Red Cross?

Safi Who?

Paula Have you called them?

Safi Me? I'm a refugee.

Paula She's fucking soaking. Come on. Let's find you something warm to wear.

Paula leaves with Little Amal.
   Derek follows Mohammed on.

Derek On behalf of my country, I am so sorry.

Mohammed You don't have to apologise.

Derek It's a shame on us. But what you're building here . . . How is it organised?

Mohammed People work together. Community elders meet to discuss problems.

Derek Incredible.

Mohammed But the problems are great.

Derek This is a city.

Mohammed I have not heard this word about Zhangal before.

Derek What did you call it?

Mohammed Zhangal.

Derek Jungle?

   Pause.

   'Now this is the Law of the Jungle, and the Law
      runneth forward and back,
   The strength of the Pack is the Wolf, and the strength
      of the Wolf is the Pack.'

Mohammed You must be very tired.

Derek Although short, the journey has been long. I feel I've been on a path here my entire life.

   Sam enters, filming everything with his phone.

Sam (*narrating*) I'm standing inside the Jungle refugee and migrant camp in Calais, France. Easy to find. Less than an hour on the Eurostar, taxi from the station.

He wouldn't come all the way so I walked the last ten minutes. It's a big area, sand dunes, along a motorway to the port. Thousands of people. Tents, a few makeshift shacks. I was expecting more police. More authority. But there don't seem to be any checkpoints at all –

Yasin No photos!

Yasin snatches Sam's phone. The phone is instantly traded, and traded again. Suddenly lots of people are involved.

Sam I'm sorry. If I just could have my phone back, please, I'll delete it, I'll give you money –

Safi Norullah!

Safi buys the phone off Norullah and hands it to Sam, who offers to repay him. Safi declines the offer.

Ask before you take someone's photo.

The music is getting louder.

Norullah (*Pashto, to Safi, about Beth*) You think she will take me to UK?

Safi (*Pashto*) I don't know. Ask her.

Norullah (*Pashto*) You ask her!

Safi (*Pashto*) No, I'm not asking her.

Norullah (*Pashto*) Go on, just ask her, just ask her.

Safi (*Pashto*) No, no, no! (*To Beth.*) Excuse me.

Norullah No!

Safi Norullah would like to ask you a question.

Beth OK!

Norullah You . . .

He mimes driving a car.

Beth I . . . what?

Norullah Car?

Beth Oh, yes. I have a car.

Norullah Me, small. I . . . English no good. (*Pashto, to Safi.*) I could hide in the back.

Safi He says he could hide in the back.

Beth I don't understand.

Safi He says he could hide in the back of the car and then you could drive him to UK.

Beth Oh . . .

Norullah Please.

Beth No . . .

Norullah Please!

Beth No, I'm so sorry, Norullah. I can't do that.

Norullah Why?

Beth How can I explain this? Car is bad. Police look inside. Police arrest me. You understand?

He looks to Safi.

Safi (*Pashto*) Sorry, my friend. She says no.

Norullah Big problem!

Sam (*to Beth*) Hey! I'm Sam.

Beth Beth!

Sam What the fuck?

Beth I know, right?!

Sam Insane.

Beth It's like –

Sam Glastonbury –

Beth Or something.

Sam Without the toilets.

Beth Yeah . . .

Sam How long have you –

Beth Four days. You?

Sam Four days. It's –

Sam *and* **Beth** Incredible.

Sam I've never met –

Beth The stories –

Sam What are you going to do?

Beth Do?

Sam I'm thinking about housing. There are big opportunities here.

Derek I'll put you in touch with Help Refugees. They're a young grassroots organisation working with MSF on a shelter model. I'm Derek.

Sam That'd be great. Sam.

Beth I met them. They're brilliant. Beth.

Derek Hi, Beth. Have you seen the warehouse for donations?

Sam Just –

Sam *and* **Beth** Amazing.

Beth Housing is a really good idea.

Sam You think?

Beth I mean, it's sort of OK now, but –

All Winter.

Beth *and* **Derek** With the wind –

All From the sea.

Sam I know.

Paula enters with Little Amal, who is wearing new clothes.

Derek Things are going to get really awful. The people here need to organise, politically.

Paula Tell me you're from a major NGO.

Derek I'm from Reading.

Paula Halle-fucking-lujah. Paula.

Derek Derek.

Sam Sam.

Beth Beth.

Norullah Norullah.

Beth I think I'm going to build a school.

Safi A school?

Sam Shit. A school is a great idea.

Beth I think it's the first idea I've ever had.

Boxer enters with Helene, playing his banjo and singing. A raucous duet.

Boxer *and* **Helene**
'Now, I'm the King of the swingers
Oh, the Jungle VIP!
I've reached the top and had to stop
And that's what's bothering me!

'Oh, oobee doo
I wanna be like you
I wanna walk like you
Talk like you
You'll see it's true
An ape like me
Can learn to be human too!'

Helene pushes him away in fits of giggles, and he finds the other volunteers.

Boxer Tell you what, those Eritreans know how to put it away! One euro for a can of Petroburg? Pints haven't been this cheap since I were thirteen! Boxer, Boxer, Boxer, Boxer. Nice to meet you, nice to meet you. Lots of newbies here, then. Choose your adjective: shocking, shameful, appalling, galling, dirty, awful, but oh so inspiring. I've been here since last Monday. Hitched a ride from Toon, ex wouldn't lend me her car. Snuck on a ferry. They don't check coming this way. Twenty pounds for an extra passenger? Don't think so! Get out, get lost, find this. Half an hour, I'm chilling with a set of Pakistanis, some Afghan squidge and banging on the willy banjo.

Paula Jesus Christ.

Boxer No, it's Boxer, like the workhorse. I'm here to fix stuff. I can fix anything designed before 1890. After that it gets complicated. I've got a theory, right. Everyone here is running from something. We're all refugees. So the game is, what you running from? I'll go first.

Paula Here we go.

Boxer Missus is a dragon. Custody of the bairn. Always will have because she's a fucking lawyer, fucking minted. Dragging me through pits for child support. Doesn't let me see her. And I bloody love that girl, my Lottie. So that's why I'm here. Fleeing the authoritarian regime of my ex-wife. Refugee. How's about you?

Derek Boxer, we were just speaking about –

Boxer No, come on. What you running away from, matey?

Derek I don't feel I'm running away. I'm running towards.

Boxer Ah, towards what?

Derek Community. I've found things here that have disappeared in Britain.

Boxer Not happy at home?

Derek I think we'd all agree our country has changed. People don't talk to each other.

Boxer There you go. Refugee. What about you, little miss? Shouldn't you be in school?

Beth I've finished actually.

Boxer Haven't got a job? Uni?

Beth One day, maybe.

Boxer Gap year?

Beth Sort of.

Boxer What's wrong with uni?

Beth Three years of my life. Seventy grand of debt. For what? I just felt everything was sort of shit.

Boxer Refugee. What about you, son?

Sam It's terribly important to be able to see and understand different cultures –

Boxer Jesus, say no more! Keep that silver spoon in your mouth, you'll have someone's eye out. Refugee. Thou, my darling?

Paula Getting away from wankers like you.

Boxer Orf, giggity. I'll come back to you. What about you, mate?

Safi The civil war in Syria.

Boxer Yeah, that'd do it. Refugee.

The volunteers are alone in the centre, the residents looking at them. There is a strange, brief moment: 'us' and 'them'. Norullah breaks it by pulling Beth into a dance, which sparks off the whole restaurant.
Salar walks into the centre, rips Boxer's can of beer away.

Salar Everybody out!

Boxer Oy!

Salar No drinking in my restaurant!

Everyone leaves, apart from the elders.

Now we have a problem. The British.

Mohammed What about them?

Helene They are so funny.

Salar What are they doing here?

Helene They want to help.

Salar Why?

Mohammed 'None of you will be a believer until he loves for his brother what he loves for himself.'

Salar You use the Prophet's words? They are not believers!

Helene They follow Jesus Christ. Do for others like you want them to do for you. It's no different.

Salar They do not follow Christ! I've seen more of them in your nightclub than your church.

46

Helene They might not be Christian but they can dance.

Salar We're not here to dance. And we don't need help.

Mohammed Before, there was not enough of anything.

Salar Enough to survive.

Helene For you, maybe. It's nice to afford food from restaurants. Eritreans have nothing.

Salar Hunger is good. It gets us to UK.

Ali A funny idea for the restaurant man.

Salar I suppose you like them?

Ali Actually, I agree with you.

Salar A miracle!

Ali We do not need them.

Salar Thank you.

Ali But we may want them. Have the boy count your takings. Then tell me you don't want them.

Salar Have you forgotten why we're here? We eat for UK, sleep for UK, shit for UK. We need quiet for this, and darkness. Our people think they will help them get to UK. They won't. They don't care about that.

Helene I spoke with a woman who says people in UK don't know what is happening here.

Salar You believe this?

Helene If they know, maybe the border will open.

Salar They know.

Mohammed This is a good chance for us. A lady wants to build a library. There are plans for a children's centre. Real wooden houses –

Salar I have heard there may be a theatre for entertainment.

Mohammed All of these things are important.

Salar Important for what? For who?

Salar sees Norullah leaving.

Where are you going?

Norullah Miss Beth builds school.

Salar takes him, stands him on the table in front of everyone.

Salar This boy is a refugee. He is a soldier. He is a warrior. He is Afghanistan. His father was killed by the Taliban. He walked here. He builds this place with me. He buys food from the shop every day. He provides for all the people of Zhangal. This boy does not need a school. He needs UK. And, inshallah, he will get this.

All Inshallah.

Helene So what are you saying, Salar? We kick them out?

Salar Yes.

Helene How do we do this?

Salar We tell them, go! You are not wanted.

Norullah tries to get down, Salar keeps him standing on the table.

Ali You are not the border man, Salar.

Helene Salar deports from Zhangal!

Mohammed When I arrive in UK I hope for welcome. Now we should offer the same.

Safi We must come to a decision about this. A vote.

Salar Vote?

Safi Everyone can give their mind.

Salar We do not vote. We agree.

Ali Agree with you?

Salar Yes.

Mohammed No, this is a good idea. There is disagreement, so we vote.

Safi Do we accept help of British man? Do we welcome him? Who says yes?

Helene, Ali and Mohammed raise their hands. Salar does not.

Salar?

Salar I do not.

Safi We must have an agreement, my friend.

Salar I know what British are like. They go to places they don't belong and tell people what to do. They have done so in Afghanistan many times. Not here. Not in Zhangal.

Helene Jungle, they call it.

Salar What did she say?

Safi They have started calling it the Jungle.

Salar So already they make us animals. If they stay, they support us in everything. They do not decide. They do not tell us what to do.

Safi (*to everyone*) First they stayed one night. Then they stayed two nights. Then they moved in . . .

FOUR

THE GOLD RUSH

Derek opens the first full meeting of the Jungle.

Derek Welcome, salam, darood, to the first democratic meeting in the history of the Jungle! I am Derek, I have come from the UK to stand in solidarity with you. Safi and I will chair these meetings. They are a safe space where all voices can be heard. We have organised translators for all languages of the camp. I only ask that we are respectful towards one another. Translations, please!

Translations.

Now, I want to thank everyone for suggestions for our first agenda. We have education, housing, distributions, drinking water –

Norullah Place for shit!

Derek Yes, sanitation is on here. Police violence, wi-fi and . . . green energy. There's a lot to get through.

Yasin UK? Wanna talk about UK!

Cheers of 'UK! UK! UK!'

Derek Perhaps we can save UK for any other business? Now, I wanted to start with a thought I've been having. The name of this place, our temporary home. It does not feel like a jungle to me.

Maz Jungle for animals, not for humans!

Derek Yes, it's a town. A thriving, bubbling town. A town of hope. So I want to propose we change it. A new name!

Cheers.

A more fitting name!

Cheers.

Hope Town!

Silence.

I'll leave that there. Have a think, I'll put it on the
agenda for next time. Who's first?

Salar I will speak. I would like to say thank you to
British man for coming here. Already you have been great
help. Now is like gold rush in the Jungle! I know it can
be difficult to treat all nationalities equally. But I know
you will find ways of being fair. And of maintaining
peace in the Jungle. Thank you, British man!

He starts to clap, some others join.

Derek Thank you, Salar. Now let me see what we have –

Paula I'll go. Paula. Women and Children's Centre.
Thank you, Boxer, for the building. Hasn't blown away
yet. Women's distribution on Monday, kid's distribution,
Wednesday. And I know we're all getting on our fucking
high horses here about all sorts of shit, but send the kids
to me. No one else is looking after them. Fuck knows
where Save the Children are. Certainly not saving the
fucking children. Help Refugees are working with
Citizens UK and Safe Passage on a law called Dublin III.
Remember the name. It gives all unaccompanied children
who have family in Europe the right to be reunited with
them. Legally. *In* a Eurostar, not on top of it. Britain
signed it –

Cheers.

France signed it.

Norullah Fuck France!

Paula It is, what you might call, a law. Trouble is,
Theresa darling buds of fucking May doesn't give a shit.

51

Norullah Fucking May shit!

Paula So, if you meet a child who's on their own, send them to the centre. We will get them to safety. And if anyone sees little darling Jamil, tell him to give my fucking phone back. End of speech.

She leaves to applause from the refugees.

Derek Alright. Thank you, Paula. Next on the agenda: Beth's school.

Beth's school. No desks, chairs, just a big open space.

Beth OK, very good. Let's start again. Back to the present.

Norullah We climb up top to lorry roof, then cut.

Beth What with?

Norullah Have knife. This word, the thing we cut?

Beth The canvas?

Norullah Canvas. Then climb to hole.

Beth Climb *through* the hole.

Norullah Climb *through* the hole, then take from shoes.

Beth Take what from shoes?

Helene The strings!

Beth The laces? Why?

Norullah For tie up hole!

Yasin. To stop the light come in when police have search!

Beth Have you all done this?

All. Yes!

Beth God. What happens next?

Omar We hide.

Beth Where?

Norullah Box.

Beth In the box?

Norullah Yes, we hide inside the box! Box farest from door.

Beth Furthest.

Norullah Oh, shit! Yes, good. *Furthest* from the door.

Beth Why the furthest?

Norullah So police don't find!

Beth You hide yourself inside the box furthest from the door –

Norullah No!

Beth Go on . . .

Norullah My friend from Afghanistan –

Maz I am friend!

Norullah He . . .

Yasin. He hided you.

Beth He hid you. It's an . . .

All. Exception!

Beth Hid is the past tense. But we're still in the present. So . . .

Norullah So . . . he hides me . . .

Beth Because?

Norullah Because, I can't hide myself!

Beth All together, from the start.

She points at each of them in turn.

Norullah I cut the canvas with my knife –

Omar I climb through hole –

Yasin I tie the hole with shoe laces –

Maz – and my friend from Afghanistan –

Helene – hides me inside a box –

Maz – furthest from the door –

Norullah – because I can't hide myself!

Beth Now we're getting somewhere! Write that down.

Sam (*to Beth*) Do you always teach in those leggings?

Beth What's wrong with my leggings?

Sam Nothing. Just that some of the other female
volunteers cover their arms, legs. Saw a girl from
Chiswick basically arrive in a burka.

Beth I don't really think about it, to be honest. But I'm
glad you are. Thanks.

Sam I'm not having a go.

Beth No, I know.

Sam Just interested.

Beth I'm glad you see me as a female volunteer.

Sam Not just that.

Beth While we're on clothing, you should ditch the
Barbour jacket. This isn't *Monarch of the Glen*. (Back to
the class.) OK, what next?

Maz Because come the box.

Helene No, the box comes –

Maz The box comes down like . . .

Norullah Like this. He pushes the box on the box!

Beth Another box?

Norullah Yes!

Beth And then what happens?

Norullah And then he –

Helene Closes the door!

Beth What door? I thought you came in through a hole!

Norullah This is different try. We try five times each night!

Helene Keep up, Miss Beth!

Beth Sorry! So your friend closes the door.

Norullah Not my friend. My friend –

Maz Hello!

Norullah He is inside the lorry.

Maz I am inside lorry!

Helene Everyone knows you can't lock lorry door from inside lorry.

Maz I think Miss Beth has never try!

Beth So who closes the door?

Omar Man!

Beth Do you pay the man?

Norullah No, no, not smuggler, he is helped me.

Beth He what? Present tense.

Norullah He is helping me.

Beth Complete the sentence.

Norullah He is helping me hide inside the lorry!

Beth Why does he help you?

Helene We take in turns each night to help.

Norullah And tomorrow I help him.

Safi enters with Okot.

Safi Beth, I have a new student for you.

Beth jumps out the box. Norullah eyes Okot.

Beth Great! What's your name?

Okot doesn't respond.

Safi He's called Okot.

Beth Nice to meet you, Okot. We're telling a story. We've cut the canvas of a lorry, climbed through the hole, and hid inside a box, and that's where we are at the moment. What happens next, Norullah?

Norullah stares at Okot.

Come on! I want to hear.

Norullah Lorry drive, is drive long way. I think this is good chance!

Yasin Then lorry stops.

Norullah I hear the door.

Maz Torch shines in.

Omar Box lid opens.

Beth Oh no! Who is it?

Helene Police!

Norullah But special police. He looks at me and smiles –

Beth What do you think happens next, Okot?

Okot I don't understand.

Beth What does the policeman say?

Okot He say, 'Go back to Jungle, no chance.'

Norullah He said, fuck you!

Beth Norullah, no. Okot is our policeman. What happens next? This time, past tense.

Norullah Oh, shit. D, d, d.

Beth You can do it.

Norullah Same night –

Beth The same night -

Norullah The same night, I got in different lorry. But this time I use my mind.

Okot Used.

Norullah Fucking D! Used. D. D. I can't do fucking past!

Beth The past is hard, but you can do it.

Helene Everyone goes for the furthest box.

Norullah But I went for the nearest. Lorry drived –

Okot Drove. The lorry drove.

Beth Good, Okot! It's an –

All Exception!

Norullah Mother fuck exception, fucking black man fucking –

Norullah goes for Okot and they fly into a brawl.
Beth tries to separate them but is hit by a stray hand.

Safi pulls them apart. Norullah runs out. Okot's face is bleeding.

Safi Everyone out.

Beth Okot, you stay.

The school empties.

Shit.

Beth, Okot and Safi are left.

I've got a first-aid kit.

Sam (*now wearing a bright yellow raincoat, to Beth*) Going well?

Beth Oh, you know. We fight, we fought, we will fight. Nice jacket. (To Okot.) How long have you been here?

He doesn't respond.

Safi Two months.

Beth Your age?

He doesn't respond.

Safi He says he's twenty.

Beth Your real age?

Okot Seventeen.

She shakes her head.

This is the life we have.

Beth Are you here by yourself?

Okot My uncle has good chance. He is in Leicester.

Beth Does everyone have an uncle in Leicester?

Okot smiles.

This will hurt.

She cleans the cut. Okot flinches.

Your English is really good. You should be teaching me.

Okot My mother taught me.

Beth She's a teacher?

Okot She lives with books. She always tells me words are so important. I learn for her.

Beth She's right.

She sticks a plaster on his cut, Okot flinches, and she notices bruising down his neck.

Have you been trying every night?

Okot Yes.

Beth I can tell. Your neck is . . .

Okot My whole body. Not just from trying. This is from long time.

Pause.

Beth Have you thought about claiming asylum here?

Okot Why would I do this?

Beth France is a good country.

Okot You think this is good country?

Beth The Jungle isn't France. There are lots of great cities. You'd be able to go to school. Music school. If you want, we could go and speak to a legal person –

Okot gets up and moves away from her.

Okot I have one dream.

Beth Tell me.

Okot You can help.

Beth Oh, I'm sorry. That's the one thing I can't help you

59

with.

Okot See. I stand on the beach and see the white cliffs. Give me your phone.

Beth looks to Safi for guidance.

Safi It's up to you.

She hands Okot her phone. He types in his number then calls his own phone and saves her number.

Beth Come back tomorrow?

Okot Not if this crazy Afghan is here.

Beth He will be. But I want you to come back.

Okot God willing, tonight I have good chance.

Beth Inshallah.

Okot Salutations, Miss Beth.

He leaves.
Sam spreads a big map of the Jungle across the floor.

Sam What do you think?

Beth Have you actually built any houses yet?

Sam Nearly.

Beth What's Quadrant 4?

Sam South, along Route des Gravelines.

Beth Kurdistan?

Sam No, it's an area where some Kurdish people live.

Beth So it's Kurdistan.

Sam It's an area populated principally by Kurdish people.

Beth Otherwise known as Kurdistan.

Sam But where does Kurdistan end and Iran begin?

Beth Sounds like Kurdistan to me.

Sam It's imprecise.

Beth The world's imprecise.

Sam Look, I've divided my map into quadrants. The area of the Jungle where lots of Kurdish people live, which is also an area where some Iranians live, as well as a few Pakistanis, Palestinians and several caravans of people from Peckham, that is Quadrant 4.

Beth Quadrant 4, with its unique and ancient culture.

Sam If it's called Kurdistan there are tensions. It has to be objective.

Derek (*to the meeting*) Housing distribution.

Sam hands out copies of his map.

Sam This is my methodology for distributing houses. I have considered many factors, of which nationality is only one. I've done a very basic count of the areas, by tents. This is the map I've made. I'm estimating the Sudanese are the largest population –

Salar Afghanistan is the largest.

Mohammed We don't know that, Salar.

Sam Let's say they're equivalent?

Salar They're not.

Ali Where is Kurdistan?

Sam It isn't on there.

Ali You don't recognise State of Kurdistan?

Sam No. I mean, yes. I'm grouping it with Iraq and Iran, in this quadrant here –

Ali You're doing what?

Sam Or not . . .

Ali Do you have any idea of our history?!

Sam None of the nationalities are on there –

Derek OK, shall we move on to the next item? Food hygiene!

Beth (*to Sam*) Going well?

Sam Be nice.

Beth What school did you go to?

Sam Is it relevant?

Beth Maybe.

Sam Eton. I went to Eton.

Beth No! Did you actually?

Sam Don't say it like that. This isn't me coming out.

Beth It is relevant. I've never met anyone from Eton before. Do we shake hands or . . .?

Sam Shut up.

Beth Do I kiss your feet?

Sam You kiss my ass.

Derek (*to the meeting*) Sam has a new proposition for housing.

Sam OK, Kurdistan is Kurdistan. Afghanistan, Sudan, Syria, Eritrea, Iraq, Iran. And then the smaller nationalities – Kuwait, Egypt, Somalia and so on. We will distribute in proportion. So, if I can build one hundred houses a day, let's say, I'll start by building twenty in Afghanistan –

Salar Good.

Sam And twenty in Sudan.

Mohammed Yes.

Sam Ten each in Syria, Eritrea, Iraq, Iran, Kurdistan. And the remaining ten for the smaller nationalities. Any questions? Good. The second factor I've considered is need. This falls under five sub-categories. Gender, age, illness or disability, time spent in the Jungle and the condition of your current dwelling. So, a woman with children will generally be housed before a single man, but a single man who has been here for five months, who has scabies, whose tent is flooded, may get a house before a single woman. Does that make sense?

Derek It's very good, Sam.

Sam I've weighted it. It's like an algorithm.

Helene Algorithm?

Sam Sorry, it's an English word.

Safi It's an Arabic word, actually.

Sam It's an Arabic word that means formula. An equation.

Ali What happens when the owner of a house has good chance?

Sam It's reallocated to someone living in that person's quadrant. Sorry, country.

Mohammed How many houses can you build?

Sam Right now, I'm on six a day. But if I can rely on all of your help, there's no reason I can't build a hundred.

Helene How will they be built?

Sam I've streamlined production. We buy materials in bulk now, which saves money. The design is good. Pallets for the base. Four walls with insulation. Sloping roof and waterproof canvas. We build the shelters in flat-pack off-site because it speeds up production. Most of you are better builders than we are, so we bring the pieces in and you put them together yourselves.

Boxer enters.

Salar What is he doing here?

Sam Boxer has offered to lead on assembly on-site.

Boxer I've got a drill with sixteen bits, hammer, an axe, chainsaw and a screwdriver. Made the mistake of lending my spanner to an Afghan and you can all guess what happened there.

Salar shouts in disgust.

I have conditions. I don't like talking on the job, especially in languages I don't understand. You want to chat, I'll meet you in the bar after and once I'm there I'm golden. But, at the end of the day, we're not here because we like each other. We're here because we have to be. Either because we've been forced or because we have a duty. So that's that really. And if you have any complaints, there's no grievance policy or shite like that. Just bugger off and get on with it. And don't touch my fucking tool box.

Derek Thank you, Boxer.

Salar I am not happy that the drunk man builds our houses.

Beth (*to Sam*) Why are you here?

Sam What does that mean?

Beth Don't see any other Eton folk round these parts.

Sam You've not been to the Eton area? It's just beneath the motorway, between Kurdistan and the portaloos.

Beth Quadrant 5? You haven't told your parents you're here.

Beth's phone goes off. She doesn't recognise the number, rejects.

Sam What have you told yours?

Beth That I'm running a school in the Jungle.

Sam And they don't mind?

Beth They love it! My mum does bun sales. Where do they think you are?

Sam Tutoring an oligarch's son in Lyon.

Beth Jesus. Thank God I'm not posh. They'd be really proud of you.

Derek (*to the meeting*) I think this system will work.

Sam This system *will* work.

Salar You will face many problems. There are tensions here. Old wars.

Sam It's really quite complicated organising something like this. Fundraising, volunteers, vans, without . . . all of that.

Salar You ask us to forget?

Sam To be honest, it would be really helpful if you could.

Mohammed We are friends here.

Salar One day I will tell you about my village in Afghanistan. You have destroyed it three times in the last two hundred years.

Mohammed Leave him alone, Salar.

Sam I've never destroyed your village.

Salar Your army has.

Sam *My* army?

Helene While you are all arguing, many Eritrean women are still in tents. The only protection we have is a whistle from Paula. We need strong wooden houses with doors and locks. We need this now. Not more problems.

She leaves.

Mohammed When can we see your algorithm, Sam?

Sam You can't.

Salar Why not?

Sam It's in my head.

Pause.

Mohammed How do we find you?

Sam Look for the yellow coat.

Derek Alright, good progress on housing. Now, is there any other business?

Maz We have heard the border will open on 21st October. What can we do to prepare?

Derek I'm not sure . . .

Yasin Border opens?

Maz Yes, Mr David Cameron decides.

Loud cheers.

Derek Now, wait. Just hold on –

Yasin How is we not know this?! Who told you!

Derek Please, everyone –

Norullah We go UK!

Derek No! The border will not be opened in October.

Maz What day?

Derek Not any day. I don't know where you heard this, but it absolutely isn't true. Safi?

Safi Derek means it is rumour. A false rumour that has spread.

Anger rises.
  Car horns beep from the motorway.

Derek Please, this is a safe space!

Yohannes Dugar! Dugar!

Everyone rushes out.

Derek We still need to action . . .

Boxer What the hell was that?

Salar Dugar.

Safi Traffic jam on the motorway.

Boxer Fucking classic. Got to see this!

Derek Well, I thought that was the best so far.

FIVE
THE TEST

Safi When does a place become a place? By November in the Jungle I could walk from Sudan through Palestine and Syria, pop into a Pakistani café on Oxford Street near Egypt, buy new shoes from the marketplace, Belgian cigarettes from an Iraqi corner shop, through Somalia, hot naan from the Kurdish baker, passing dentists, Eritrea, distribution points, Kuwait, hairdressers and legal centres, turn left on to François Hollande Street, stop at the sauna, catch a play in the theatre, mass at the church, khutba in a mosque, before arriving at Salar's restaurant in Afghanistan. When does a place become home?

Night time. It's Salar's birthday. A cake is lit, and everyone sings.

Derek Do you remember the gentleman in the tweed jacket who ate here last week? It was A.A. Gill, restaurant reviewer for the *Sunday Times*, newspaper of record of the Great British Isles. And his review is just out.

Mohammed unveils a beautiful framed copy of the review.

Take it away, Mohammed.

Mohammed 'The room is a tent –

A cheer. Cheers throughout the speech.

– with a make-do kitchen in one corner, a couple of gas rings, a banged-together counter, a kettle, some pots and pans . . . The dishes come hot and generous, with fluffy, nutty white rice. The red beans are a great, solid, aromatic dose . . . as warm and uncomplicated as a hug. The surprise, the great surprise, is the chicken livers. They are perfect . . . like earth and grass and licked copper. The sauce is pungently hot . . . This was a properly, cleverly crafted and wholly unexpected dish, made with a finesse that defied the surroundings, but at the same time elevated them . . .'

Mohammed hands it to Salar.

Happy Birthday, my friend.

Salar Four stars for atmosphere –

A huge cheer.

And four stars for the food!

Norullah Eight stars!

Salar I have five on TripAdvisor.

Norullah Thirteen stars!

'Hip, hip, hoorays', and calls for a speech.

Salar Alright, thank you, thank you. I don't know how you all found out –

Norullah I told them!

Salar Yes. My restaurant man. Something funny. In Afghanistan many people do not know their birthday. Because of the wars, no one kept records. So, and this is true, I have . . . I had thirty-seven friends who all have birthday on January 1st. But I am lucky. My mother wrote it down! This is maybe the strangest place I have celebrated my birthday. And the strangest group of friends. But friends. That's all. Now get out my restaurant! There is a border to cross!

All Yayayayayayayaya!

Paula (*to Boxer*) You alright?

Boxer It's my little one's birthday, an' all.

Paula Why didn't you go back?

Boxer Can't afford the ferry. The ex wouldn't have me anyway.

Paula You barmy bugger. You haven't called her, have you?

Boxer Lost my phone. Call this a fucking father?

Paula Use this.

She gives him her phone.

You're doing well, love. Stay out the Eritrean nightclub, yeah? Call her now.

Boxer Cheers, Paula. You're a diamond.

Sam (*to Beth*) Do you want to stay in a hotel tonight?

Beth Sorry?

Sam A nice hotel. Nice-ish.

Beth Erm . . .

Sam Hear me out. We've been sleeping in tents for three months. My back's stiff –

Beth What's stiff?

Sam I've had the same stone in my spine for too long. I say nice-ish hotel, TV, the World Service, wi-fi – remember that? Maybe a bottle of wine –

Beth I'm quite at home, thanks.

Sam Room service? The option of having a bloody bath? There we are. You know you want a bath. I can see it in your eyes.

Beth No, you can't.

Sam We don't have to share a bed or anything, if that's –

Beth Say that again?

Sam I just mean, we can get a room with lots of beds. Three beds. Four beds, even! We can keep swapping in the night.

Beth Swapping?

Sam Forget it!

Beth receives a call. She answers.

Beth Hello?

Sam I'll go back to my tent.

Beth Where?

Sam And my stone.

Beth OK, stay calm.

Sam My cold, hard stone.

Beth Don't say anything. Don't do anything. I'm coming.

Sam What is it?

Beth Okot He's been arrested.

Outside the detention centre.

Guard Oui?

Beth Hello, I'm looking for a boy. He was arrested a few hours ago.

Guard This is France, you speak French.

Beth OK . . . *Je suis . . . en train de . . . trouver quelqu'un.*

Guard British?

Beth *Oui. Je suis ici pour . . . voir un . . . jeun garçon.*

Guard No.

Beth He's not in here.

Safi He is. Ask again.

Beth *Il est soudanais . . . Il est détenu ici . . . Il a dix-sept ans.*

Guard *Nom?*

Beth Okot Sherif.

Guard *Pardon?*

Beth Okot Sherif.

Guard *Non, comment vous appelez-vous?*

Beth Oh. Bethan James.

He leaves.

Est-il ici? Je dois le voir maintenant.

He returns with Okot, who is obviously injured.

Guard *Dix minutes.*

The Guard leaves them.

Beth Okot, what the fuck? What happened?

He doesn't respond.

Have they asked how old you are?

Safi He said he's twenty.

Beth What? Why did you say that?!

Safi If they think he's a child, they will keep him in France.

Beth Have you signed anything?

Safi They gave him a document.

Beth In French?

Okot nods.

Did you have a translator, a lawyer?

Safi That must be a joke.

Beth Did you sign it? Okot?

Okot Yes.

Beth Why would you do that?

The Guard re-enters.

Guard You must go now.

Beth We're not finished, you said ten minutes.

Guard There is problem. You must leave.

Beth This is madness!

Guard *Maintenant!*

Beth I'm not leaving!

Guard You are in France, you speak French!

Beth This is not France! He's a seventeen-year-old boy! Look at him! This is not France! You've forced him to sign documents! He doesn't speak French! He should have a translator, that's the *law*. This is *not France*. I have friends. Lawyers. Human rights lawyers. In Paris. And if I call them they are going to hit you so hard. No translator, forced to sign, seventeen years old, cuts, bruises all over his body. Where did he get those? There's a European Convention on the Rights of the Child, don't you dare say this is France! I'm serious. Look at me. I will make your life hell. We're walking out of here today, now. I don't care what he's signed. You're going to rip it up and let him go.

Guard looks her up and down.

Guard OK.

Beth Excuse me?

Guard Go! And if I see him again, you won't.

They step out of the detention centre.

Beth Fuck. I don't know anyone in Paris.

Pause. She looks at Okot.

Do you want to stay in a hotel tonight?

The Hotel Meurice.

Safi You know it's illegal to stay in a hotel without papers.

Beth I know.

Safi And it's against the law in France to aid refugees.

Beth Yeah, thanks, Safi.

Beth and Okot enter a room.

Right, let's get you cleaned up. (*As she goes into the bathroom to get a bowl of water.*) Were you trying on the trains? You should be careful on the trains, people die on the trains.

Okot is left alone with Safi.

Safi Do you want to talk? Talking sometimes helps.

Okot If I talk to her. You think she would understand?

Pause.

Safi I think she could.

Pause. Okot takes his top off. He has scars, old and new, all over his body.

Talk to her. Tell her.

Beth re-enters.

Beth Oh, fuck. Oh, my God.

Pause.

Okot I am dead.

Beth What?

Okot Dead.

Beth You're not dead. You're here with me.

Okot Dead. A refugee dies many times.

74

Beth I know –

Okot You know?

Beth I didn't mean that. I mean I can imagine.

A long pause.

Okot What do you know of me?

Beth You're from Sudan.

Okot Where?

Beth Darfur?

Okot What do you know of Darfur?

Beth There are lots of problems in Darfur.

Okot What problems?

Beth A genocide . . . When . . . an entire people is . . .

Okot A people?

Beth A race or religion. When a people is –

Okot People is your father. People is your mother. What do you know about the Mediterranean?

Beth I know about the boats.

He is silent. She is forced to continue. She is uneasy.

The boats are small. Too many people are put inside. By the smugglers. Lots of people, lots of the boats sink. It's obviously really dangerous.

Okot Yes . . .

Beth Hundreds of people try to cross every day. It's tragic.

Silence.

It's a tragedy.

Silence.

I don't know.

Okot Sahara is more dangerous. You are in a truck six days and six nights. If truck breaks down, you die. If you fall out, you die. If you run out of water, you die. If militia find you, you die. If you don't keep warm at night, you die. If you die in the Sahara your body is never found. If I die in the Sahara, my body is never found. Six days, six nights.

Beth Did you do it alone?

Okot I survive with my uncle.

Safi He thought he was his uncle.

Okot I have never been this far from my mother . . . I cannot be boy any more . . . First death. You know about Libya.

Beth No . . .

Okot You must know about Libya! Everyone about Libya say same thing: Libya is worst place in world! Everyone has gun. Big problems for black people. But at least we are here. One step further.

Beth That's good.

Safi Go on.

Okot In Tripoli you look for a middle man.

Safi You know this word? Middle man.

Okot He takes you to the smuggler. The smuggler pays him. And you pay the smuggler. Some people pay $2,000. We pay $400. I thought this was fair! Pay what you can! I thought we go to harbour. But no. They send us to mazraa.

Safi Compound. Warehouse.

Okot It is prison. Out of city. Nowhere away. You know it as maybe . . . (*To Safi, Arabic.*) Hell?

Safi Hell.

Okot Mazraa. They keep you. Two months, maybe. Little food, little water. Shit-place in corner. Torture. I have seen men do to the teeth. Slice this muscle on thumb. Flip coin to choose which toe. And other things you *cannot* know.
   I lose my uncle here also . . . I get to know my uncle.

Safi It's not his uncle.

Okot For women . . . it is even more difficult. You know. I know you know, because you are scared now. You are scared to think mazraa.

Safi She doesn't know. They don't know.

Okot Your mind cannot think.

Safi Do you think we'd be here if they knew?

Okot They lie me down. Lift concrete stone on my back, heavy. They make a video on my phone to send to my mother to see. I must ask her for more money. More money, more, more, more! I think of my mother . . . I think of Darfur. Darfur is the most beautiful place in the world. Have you seen the sun rise in Darfur?

Beth No.

Okot You never need to see it rise again. My mother is like librarian. She takes books around town and villages, and we sing and eat aseeda and shorbet adas, and if you are lucky a big white Nile fish from a traveller from the east. Last time I saw my mother she was crying. You've seen your mother cry?

Beth Yes.

Okot Me too. But never like this. She comes close to me, and grabs me, 'You must go,' she says. 'The men have come to look for you. Go now. Go to UK. There you will be safe.' A man arrived who I had never seen before. My mother says he is my uncle. She gives him $400. All the money she has. She has nothing more.

I think of her watching this video. She will be crying. She has nothing more. She cannot pay. I think of her watching the video.

Second death.

Pause. Okot can't continue.

Safi Finally you are taken to the boats, yes?

Okot Yes.

Safi The coastguard has been paid. The local militia. Was it a big boat?

Okot Small boat.

Safi Rubber?

Okot Yes.

Safi A Zodiac. Fifty people.

Ali You are given a package with a balloon to put your phone in, GPS device, a life jacket –

Safi You hope the life jacket is real.

Yasin You pray the life jacket is real.

Ali Real or not, fifteen dinar for package.

Okot I am in first boat.

Safi The first?

Residents of the Jungle have gathered round to listen. They look at each other, anxious.

Norullah Big problem.

Okot We go out to bigger boat.

Safi A fishing trawler. Fifteen metres long.

Ali Painted black so the coastguard can't see.

Safi Wooden. Strong. But old.

Okot The less money you pay, the worse your place on boat. Pay what you can. Now you know.

Beth Yes. Now I know.

Safi Rich people go on top deck. Poor go underneath. Below sea level. In the hold.

Okot I am pushed down near engine. It is going in my face.

Safi The Zodiacs keep coming. This boat is for a hundred people. Here there are seven hundred.

Okot People on top of people on top of people.

Maz Eighty degrees.

Yohannes Ninety degrees.

Omid A hundred.

Okot The heat is unbearable.

Safi No smugglers make this journey, do you know this? You are left alone. Point in direction and go.

Okot Stay still or boat will sink, you drown!

Ali Wait for international waters, then phone for help.

Okot Suddenly I am thinking I shouldn't be here. I try to get out. I shout. I cannot move. I hear water outside. If boat have problem I am dead. All of below, we are dead.

Helene comes forward with Amal, singing gently.

Pressed to me is mother and daughter. She maybe three years old. I think what will she remember. Mother is singing to stop tears.

People join in with their own songs.

Why is everyone singing?

Safi They are not singing. They are praying.

Okot Suddenly I am praying.

Safi If you stand on the shores at night of Lesvos or Kos, you hear this sound from the boats, like the sea itself is praying.

Okot A man cries out loud.

Mohammed comes forward.

And at moment of his most tears, he shits. He has tight teeth and is shamed for what has happened. He tries to say sorry but he cannot stop crying. A girl is sick. So another person is sick. So I am sick.

Beth Okot!

Okot Panic cause the boat to tip. The tip causes more panic. Shouts of leak. Maybe it is piss. Please be piss.

Safi It is not piss.

Norullah comes forward.

Okot Then the floor turn round and hundreds of bodies spin in the hold.

Safi Water rushes in.

Norullah A man shouts. 'Take off your shoes! Take off your shoes!'

Okot I rip my trouser off because a man is holding on

to me. Another man is pushing up against the door.

Mohammed Push! Push!

Okot The door swings out –

Salar comes forward.

Safi Five minutes he is under the water.

Okot Five minutes.

Safi Think.

Okot I am dead. Third death.

Safi recites prayer.

Real death.

Residents of the Jungle have closed around Beth.

Safi You want to ask a question.

Beth How did you survive?

Helene We didn't.

Beth But you're here now.

Okot This is not us.

Safi We're different now. New.

Okot Why are you here, Beth?

Mohammed Why are you not at your home?

Safi What can we give you?

Okot Before, I could give you anything. I could give you myself.

Helene What do we have now?

Okot This journey. This story.

Safi And you have heard this story before. A thousand

times, I am sure.

Okot Now you know. It isn't me. But now it is me.

Safi's phone rings, he gives it to Beth. She answers.
Many phones ring.

Safi Friday 13th November, terrorists murdered a
hundred and thirty people in Paris, in restaurants, a
stadium, a theatre. The deadliest attack in France since
the Second World War.

At the same time in the Jungle, a Sudanese man in his
wooden house wrapped himself in blankets and fell
asleep with a lit candle. It set fire to half of Sudan.

It was reported that the two events were connected.
They were not. It was also reported that a Syrian
passport was found with the body of one of the attackers.
It was fake. But does it matter?

In that moment, the refugee, terror, the Jungle and me,
were bound together. Alan Kurdi changed everything,
and the night of 13th November changed everything
again.

The horror I escaped had found me.

Residents of the Jungle hold a vigil for Paris.
Signs reading #Pray4Paris are lifted.
A minute of silence ends.

Derek Thank you, everyone. Safi is writing an open
letter, from all the citizens of the Jungle, condemning
the attacks –

Boxer It's got nothing to do with them.

Derek We know this –

Boxer They're running from the same people what did it!

Derek And that is what the letter will say. Mohammed.

Mohammed Thank you, Derek. The pictures I see in the
news, I recognise. It is Darfur. I know the pain. It is why

I'm here.

Salar It is the streets of Kabul.

Yasin Basra.

Ali Halabja.

Yohannes Irecha.

Mohammed Today we are all Paris. The fire means many Sudanese people are homeless. I want to thank Salar for opening his restaurant in our time of need, and the volunteers who worked through the night. Without this humanity, we would be lost.

Derek Thank you, Mohammed. Does anyone else have any reflections?

Paula Last night was an absolute clusterfuck. What happened to our plans? Why were people firefighting? Make breaks! That's it. We could have saved more homes. It's a miracle no one died here.

Derek There are lessons to learn, of course –

Paula No candles in a shanty town made of wood. This can never happen again.

Ali What about the rumours?

Helene What rumours?

Ali That the fire was not an accident. My boys saw men running up Rue de Garennes.

Helene Fascists meet on this road every night. They attack with metal bars.

Boxer Fuckers.

Ali We'll send a group of men to meet them tonight.

Derek No, no, no! Do not do that. We do not know what caused this.

Paula Things need to change. Volunteers were drunk. Booze, spliffs, fuck knows what. I'm not naming names –

Boxer Oh, fuck off, Paula!

Derek There is a time and a place. This is a test of our strength. We need to come together now.

Salar He was asleep in my restaurant while the fire was burning. Children were screaming and he was on the floor.

Paula Salar, I'll deal with him. (*Shouting.*) Get a grip or fuck off! Has anyone been to a proper UN refugee camp? They have staff. Rotas. Plans in preparation for shit like last night.

Derek This is not a UN refugee camp. This is us. And some credit is due for how we managed. Safi, can you please help –

Safi It's very important that we . . . Look, this is . . .

He hesitates. Salar takes over.

Salar This is not good enough. France is in a state of emergency. The police have more power. Last night was nearly Jungle finished.

Safi Salar, we have to be careful here –

Salar Let me speak. Refugees: remember why you are here. Good chance may soon be no chance. And volunteers.

Mohammed Don't divide us, Salar –

Salar We have trusted you with our lives. If you are here for holiday. Or because this is better than your home, leave. We do not want you. The last thing Zhangal needs is more refugees.

It starts to rain. Hard.

Paula And that's all we need.

Derek Rest, everyone. Stay dry. Stay strong. Don't lose hope. Safi, I need that letter as soon as possible.

Safi I'm collecting the signatures.

People disperse.

Sam Safi, we need to organise a meeting to plan the rebuild. Can I leave that with you?

Safi OK, Sam.

Beth Safi, I need your help. Okot . . .

Safi I know.

Beth He lost his house. I really need you.

Safi Leave it with me.

Beth leaves.

Salar (*to Norullah*) You do not go to the school any more.

Safi What?

Salar Don't get involved. (*Pashto.*) You heard me. You don't go to the school any more.

Safi is left alone, stunned, spat out.

SIX

THE RAIN

Beth My mum called yesterday in tears. She said, 'Have you heard about the boy who died on top of a train? It's so terrible, I can't stop crying.' My friend Jade at Bristol sends me emails, links to *Guardian* articles: 'Growing number of unaccompanied minors in Calais.' I get messages all the time from friends and family saying they're so *fucking* proud of me. That they're so *fucking* angry. All this anger is everywhere. And still, this . . . Look around, Sam. Look. I'm numb. What the fuck are we actually doing?

Sam Something.

Beth Okot has no one. His house burned down last night. He could have died.

Sam Thanks to you, he didn't.

Beth He might still.

Sam I can build him another one.

Beth It's not enough. I've got to get him out.

Sam That's not our responsibility.

Beth Why not?

Sam You run the school. I build houses. If we stick to that we can help.

Beth So don't actually try to change anything?

Sam If I didn't build houses, people would die.

Beth Maybe that's a good thing.

Sam Seriously?

Beth Maybe the government would be forced to act.

Sam I'm not going to let people die if I can stop it.

Beth We're just preserving it. We're part of the problem.

Sam I think you're upset.

Beth Fuck you.

Sam Maybe you should take a break. Go home for a bit.

Beth I don't need to go home! Okot can't go home!

Sam Then let's go for a weekend somewhere.

Beth It's always weekends and fucking hotels with you.

Sam Fine! What would you change? How would you solve it?

Beth Are you really asking me that question?

Sam Yes. You're Hollande. What do you do? Open the border? Let everyone through! The Jungle disappears and Okot's safe. But next week another ten thousand people arrive in Calais expecting to get across.

Beth You're being a wanker.

Sam Or don't do that, but get rid of the Jungle because, yes, it's fucking awful, and you know it. Get rid of it, straight away. Then there are ten thousand people you have to house and clothe and feed. Where do you house them? Who pays? It's expensive. There'll be uproar. And crucially, they don't want to be housed! They want to get to Britain! They're quite happy here and they won't go without a fight. Add into that the election here next year, Le Pen is doing pretty fucking well. And the referendum in six months' time, Farage is doing pretty fucking well there too. And while we're being honest, Calais is tiny! One camp in the north of France. There are sixty-five million refugees in the world! So come on! What the fuck do we do?

Beth You're asking me how to solve the refugee crisis?

Sam Yeah, I am. How would you solve the refugee crisis, Beth?

Safi enters with **Okot** *Norullah is eating a plate of food.*

Safi Talk to each other. This stops now.

Pause.

Norullah You want some food? Is good food. Not Lidl. Carrefour.

Okot They don't let us in Carrefour.

Norullah I steal from trash. Have some.

He pushes the plate towards Okot.

Your mother in Sudan? My father dead too. Taliban shoot.

He mimics a gunshot.

You here alone?

Okot Uncle has good chance.

Norullah My friend good chance too. Leaves me in Jungle. Fucking dick.

Okot Salar looks after you.

Norullah Hate Salar. He no let me go school. He make me fucking work.

Okot You get money?

Norullah Yeah, wanna see? (*Showing a big wad of notes.*) This not all.

Okot Where's the rest?

Norullah I'm not telling you, black man thief.

Okot Crazy fucking Afghan!

They smile.

Norullah Your house gone?

Okot Yeah.

Norullah Shit, man. It was big fucking fire.

Okot I've seen bigger.

Norullah Me too.

Okot I went close.

Norullah Me too. How close?

Okot Really close. I thought I would burn. Smoke was coming from my clothes.

Norullah Cool. They build you new house?

Okot I don't know yet. UK boy is shit.

Norullah Yellow coat? He no give me house. He only likes Sudan. But my tent fucking best tent in Jungle. Many plastic. Is warm at night, no wet.

Pause.

Stay with me if you want.

Okot Really?

Norullah You have to leave if my girlfriends come.

Okot You have girlfriends?

Norullah Norullah is big man. Many girlfriends. From all Europe. They visit me all time. My Turkey girlfriend I met in Istanbul. She is a come soon. My Greece girlfriend I met in Athens. Sometimes she just turn up! Girlfriends from Macedonia, Serbia, Hungaria, Germany, Paris, and sometime they all come one time! So, big problem. But yeah, you can stay.

Okot You need UK girlfriend.

Norullah One day.

Okot One day.

Norullah Soon.

Okot I'll stay with you.

Norullah Cool. Wanna go see Carrefour trash?

Okot OK.

> *They leave together.*
> *A meeting in Salar's restaurant.*

Derek Safi, we've started here.

Safi Sorry.

Derek We want to show you plans for the rebuild of Sudan.

Sam Many Sudanese people were displaced by the fire, so we're using it as an opportunity, a complete redesign. Proper town planning.

Mohammed That means wooden houses for everyone. Real streets. An access road. Show him on the map.

Sam Here, from Chemin des Dunes, right through the camp to the main entrance here.

Mohammed It will make distributions easier. Tell him about the streets.

> *Salar enters, and stays on the other side of the room.*

Sam We're excited about the streets. It's a grid plan. Every house will be numbered. And you know how bad the flooding is, so all streets will have irrigation ditches, and two layers of hardcore.

Safi Is this possible?

Sam Yes. Imagine it. Ahmed lives at Number 15, Street 6, and he suffers from an illness, we can work with MSF to take doctors and medicines right to his door by car. If he needs an ambulance, it can drive right to him. If lawyers need to talk to him, they'll know exactly where to find him. And that will be the same for everyone.

Safi Everyone in Sudan.

Sam This is the future of the Jungle.

Derek What do you think, Safi?

Safi I mean, it sounds . . . It sounds fantastic.

Salar How long will this take?

Sam Three weeks.

Salar How many volunteers?

Sam For it to work, I'll need everyone.

Salar Ah.

Sam So I can do it quickly and move on to the other areas.

Salar I see.

Derek What do you think, Salar?

Salar I am thinking how I will explain it to my people.

Mohammed Tell them we rebuild after the fire.

Salar They will say Sudanese are good builders, why do you need all this help?

Mohammed Hundreds my people lose their homes.

Salar How many Afghans still live in tents?

Sam Are you saying we shouldn't rebuild?

Salar No.

Sam What are you saying?

Salar Send some volunteers to Sudan while the rest build in the other areas.

Sam I'm not passing up this opportunity.

Salar You say opportunity like it is a good thing.

Derek It isn't good for anyone.

Salar Safi has said it. For Sudan, it is *fantastic*.

Mohammed Oh, come on, Salar!

Sam I can't work like this. He opposes everything I do.

Salar I meet Afghans every day who say they receive less food, less clothes, less houses –

Mohammed This isn't true!

Salar But they feel it. And then all they hear is 'crazy fucking Afghans'. This meeting. Did you not think I should have been invited? You are holding it in my restaurant. Everything you do affects the whole Jungle.

Sam I thought you didn't want our help.

Salar I don't. I want to be in UK. But as elder, I will speak for my people. I will make sure they are treated fairly.

Derek Safi, can you please help here?

Safi What do you want me to say, Derek? These are legitimate concerns. I can't solve every fucking problem!

Sam Tell me what you want.

Salar I want to know what I say to my people when they see only building in Sudan.

The women and children's centre. Paula, Helene and Little Amal are sorting through lots of donations.

Beth enters in a sodden raincoat.

Beth Dublin III.

Paula Nice to see you too.

Beth I need to get Okot out.

Paula Beth –

Beth He's falling apart.

Paula Not a single kid has made it over.

Beth Why not? You've been talking about it for months.

Paula Why do you think? The fucking Mayflower doesn't want them.

Beth It's got nothing to do with her. It's the law.

Paula And we are doing everything we can to fight it, believe me.

Helene If you are worried, you get him hostel –

Beth He won't. He'll run.

Paula Then you need to keep him safe here, in the Jungle, like the rest of them. Focus on the school, Beth. And yourself. Are you alright?

Beth I'm fine.

Paula You don't look it. Here, sit. Tea, drink.

Boxer appears in the doorway carrying a huge box of donations.

Boxer Where do you want this lot?

Paula One more step and I'll chop your bollocks off.

Boxer Too late. Ex has them in a jar on her mantelpiece.

Paula Think you're funny, do you? Women and Children's Centre. Clue's in the name.

Boxer I'm bloody helping you!

Paula You're atoning. Now piss off, before I turn you into glue.

Boxer Charming . . .

He drops the box and leaves.

Paula I think everyone needs to calm the fuck down.

She lights a cigarette.

Deep breath . . .

She takes a long drag.

Now, doesn't that feel better. Helene, why don't you tell Beth your news?

Helene I claim asylum in France.

Beth Wow.

Paula Finally, something to celebrate.

Beth When did you stop trying?

Helene Months. I hoped for smuggle, but since Paris price is too high. And I won't pay the other way.

Beth What do you mean?

Paula What do you think?

Beth So you're leaving the Jungle.

Helene No. In France you do not get house for a long time.

Beth You've claimed asylum but you still have to live here?

Paula Fucking ridiculous. But at least it means you won't be trying any more. No more trains or lorries. No more smugglers.

Helene I suppose.

Beth How do the smugglers work, Helene?

Helene You pay them and they take you to UK.

Beth Yeah, but how?

Helene You find the right one for you.

Beth There are different ones?

Helene Different smugglers for each nationality. Afghans for Afghans, Africans for Africans. Albanians take anyone but they are no good. Kurdish smugglers are best. Like Rolls-Royce. Five-star journey to UK.

Beth Why?

Helene They control the best areas. They have arrangements with best drivers who drive best lorries.

Beth Do you pay by cash?

Helene Of course.

Beth You carry all that money?

Helene Yes . . . You volunteers are so funny. You think we sew into the seams of our clothes? I have bank account!

Beth How do you find them?

Paula Why are you so interested?

Beth We have no idea what's actually happening here. This whole fucking crisis.

Paula Oh come on, Beth! It's only a crisis because we're calling it that. A million people, Europe shits her knickers. Population of seven hundred million, that's nought point fuck-knows per cent. Go to Jordan, quarter of people are refugees. Lebanon, it's a third. Crisis? European governments need to stop breaking the law. Then we need to stop the obsession with *helping*.

Helene You think we don't need help?

Paula Look at this place! Give people a chance, a hammer, some nails. Build a city in a day. You're better than we are. Smarter, braver. We're the ones who need fucking help.

Helene So why are you here?

Paula For the kids.

Helene And the adults?

Paula Come on, Helene, you know what I think about this.

Helene Paula thinks I made a choice.

Paula No, that's not what I think.

Helene Paula thinks I'm an economic migrant.

Little Amal groans.

Sure, my life was not about to end in Eritrea, but why should I spend it all in military service? My sister is the smartest woman, but she will never be free. She must build roads. I did not want this to happen for me –

Paula I know that!

Helene – so am I not still refugee?

Paula Not the choice to flee. The choice to come this far.

Helene You're wrong. Yes, I could have stayed in Italy. But my cousins are in UK. And I speak English. Everyone in Eritrea speaks English because UK used to run Eritrea! And do you know how refugees are treated in Italy? Like animals. But yes, Paula, I could have stayed in Italy.

Paula Helene, anyone who traipses across a desert, an ocean on a fucking lilo, will always have my support. You know that. But the kids are different.

Helene I didn't choose.

Paula They can't choose.

Helene I didn't choose!

Paula (*pointing to Amal*) She doesn't have the capacity to choose any of this.

Helene I didn't choose.

Paula If we can't even win the argument about unaccompanied kids like her, we don't stand a chance with you. That's why I'm here. To pin Mother fucking Teresa against a wall until she meets her obligations.

Beth You think the laws can solve this.

Paula I'll make sure they do.

Beth What if they can't?

Pause.

There's a journalist, James Bartholomew. What a name. He coined this phrase in a *Spectator* article about refugees. Virtue signalling. When people share opinions, or petitions, or crowdfunders online, he says all you're really doing is signalling your virtue. Proving how great you are. Not actually *doing* anything. I kid you not, within a week it had been picked up by every newspaper in the world. Everyone uses it now. The *New York Times*. The *Guardian*. It'll be in the dictionary this time next year, I guarantee it. First, I thought, what a wanker. Cynical world. What sorry state have we got into if we can't honestly express our horror at what is happening? That you can't cry at the picture of a boy, dead on a beach, without some fucker telling you you're lying. But now I hear you, Paula, tell me there's a law that might have saved him, but that the law isn't being used even though it's been agreed by everyone. Not just one law.

Loads of laws. Still he had to get on a boat that sank and killed him. Along with a lot of other people. I went on a school trip to Parliament. I stood at the dispatch box. We sat in the public gallery and watched a debate. I remember being so fucking awestruck by this incredible place with all the laws we've ever made. And now I know. It's all one big virtue signal. 'Look at us. Look at how much we care. These people have human rights! They do exist!' Until they're standing at our door, screaming for help. The French government. The British government. The United Nations. The European fucking Union. Where the fuck are you?

Pause.

If the system can't save Okot, fuck the system. Do it yourself.

She leaves.

Paula Beth! Fuck's sake. (*To Helene, who is also leaving.*) Where are you going?

Helene Carol service!

Singing starts offstage.

Paula Oh fuck, it's fucking Christmas.

Sam takes Henri on a tour of the Jungle.
  The Eritrean Women's Choir sings 'Oh Come, All Ye Faithful' loudly, offstage.

This is the Kurdish area. I've built about four hundred houses here. Afghanistan that way, Pakistan. Nearly a thousand houses. The Afghan High Street is the civic centre of the camp, where most of the restaurants and cafés are. And over there the rebuild of Sudan, we're making big progress in the design.

Henri Where is that music coming from?

Sam The church.

Pause, as Henri takes it all in.

Henri You're building a city.

Sam It's becoming organised.

Henri It's becoming permanent. You're building it to last.

Sam Because the problem is not going to disappear.

Henri They're not here because of my border, Sam. They're here because of yours. If we ripped up the treaty of Le Touquet today the Jungle would move to Dover tomorrow.

Sam This would never happen in Britain.

Henri Are you so sure about that?

Sam We all have responsibility for this.

Henri Responsibility for what? You are giving these people not only everything they need, but anything they want. You are making it appealing.

Sam Anyone who comes here and says this place is appealing has a problem.

Henri You think I'm cruel because I don't help these people in the way you want. But I don't want to go to bed thinking my actions have in any way persuaded someone in, let's say, Afghanistan to get inside a rubber boat, expecting to find happiness here. You give them false hope, Sam. Tell me, who do you think is cruel?

The singing ends.

You said in your message you have a proposition?

Sam I think we can help each other.

Henri How?

Sam By working together. Meeting and talking regularly. I'll update you on the situation in the camp and you can keep me informed about the prefecture's plans. I want to build a new area by the motorway. I need to know if it's worth the investment.

Henri How long do you think you have here?

Sam I was hoping you would tell me. At least until March.

Henri Why do you say that?

Sam You can't make people homeless in winter. That's French law.

Pause.

Henri This isn't France.

Sam Six months? A year?

Henri You're very impressive for a nineteen-year-old.

Sam What do you think?

Henri I would need to be discreet.

Sam So would I. It will be a good thing.

Sam holds his hand out. Henri shakes it.

Henri Don't build by the motorway.

Sam Why?

Henri Just, don't. That's all I can say. Joyeux Noël.

Christmas Day.
Boxer enters dressed as Father Christmas, carrying a big sack. He hands out presents.

Boxer Ho, ho, ho! Merry Calais Christmas! Ring your Jungle bells, cos Santa's on the straight and narrow. Don't leave brandy by your open fires. Ribena for me. Ribena with a little kick in it.

He gets his banjo out. Sings to the tune of 'Blaydon Races'.

It's Christmas in the Jungle, so it's time for something
    pleasant,
Court'sy of the British public, everyone's gettin'
    a present,
So forget your Christmas jumpers, hampers and your
    cotton socks,
Cos ev'ry school in ev'ry county in the country's sent
    a shoe box.

Oh, me lads, step up before it's all gone,
Pans from Pembroke, pots from Perth and gloves
    down from Glamorgan.
Hats from Hampshire, scarves from Shropshire,
    dungarees from Dorset,
Gannin' alang Chemin des Dunes, and back across
    the border!

The look upon his face, when he sees the Nike
    shoe box.
Score, I got a pair of Airs, a pair of brand new
    high tops,
He rips it up and looks inside and 'haddaway
    again!'
Finds several dozen tampons and some Nivea
    for Men!

Oh, me lads, step up before it's all gone,
Pans from Pembroke, pots from Perth and gloves
    down from Glamorgan.
Hats from Hampshire, scarves from Shropshire,
    dungarees from Dorset,
Gannin' alang Chemin des Dunes, and back across
    the border!

Listen to me, you stingy twats, if you want to help
    refugees,

I'll tell ya lot, all honesty, exactly what they do need,
Send them Adidas, Nike, iPhones, Samsungs, sim
    cards, cash and iPods,
And for pity's sake, you thoughtless prats, don't send
    them in a shoe box!

Oh, me lads, step up before it's all gone,
Pans from Pembroke, pots from Perth and gloves
    down from Glamorgan.
Hats from Hampshire, scarves from Shropshire,
    dungarees from Dorset,
Gannin' alang Chemin des Dunes, and back across
    the border!

And, I'm not kidding, someone actually sent a box of
dildos down from Durham. So that's Paula sorted. For
this year. Optimistic, to say the least. But then again,
why the fuck not?

He bursts into tears.

Christmas is about being good to each other! Appreciating
how fucking happy you really are. It's about loving your
family. It's about holding your daughter and not letting
go! It's about Lottie! I miss you to high heaven, baby.

How many of you are away from your bairns and all?
Your mums and dads? Your brothers and sisters? Bet
that makes the fucking lot of us.

There. That's it. That's Christmas. Now bugger off.
I'm going to call Lottie. Oh, and Theresa May? Open the
border, you heartless bitch. Don't you know there are
children here?

Merry fucking Christmas!

*Derek, Safi and Mohammed in a tent, late on Christmas
night. Derek is very drunk.*

Derek The paradox at the heart of the Jungle is that the
refugees are running in one direction and the volunteers

are running in another. We have met here, in this middle ground, but we are running towards the same thing! We're building an image of Britain that doesn't exist! That's never existed! Certainly not in Britain. It exists in our dreams only. But I see the beginnings of it in this place. With time, it could exist here.

Mohammed In Calais?

Derek This is not Calais. This is not France. It has changed hands so many times in the last thousand years, you wouldn't believe. There are so many claims to this land, it is claimless. So why can't we claim it?

Mohammed It is a very funny idea.

Derek They gave us this land. I know it sounds mad, but every place started somewhere, at some time.

Mohammed We could have our own currency.

Derek Jerusalem. Athens. Alexandria. London.

Mohammed Start taxing people!

Derek They were places like this once. A group of people, waiting by a river, a coast. A moment came when the waiting stopped.

Mohammed Passports and borders!

Derek This is real.

Mohammed Jungle army. We must defend ourselves!

Derek Of course, there are challenges. But we are facing them together. We can solve them. Is it really so mad?

Mohammed It is not mad to believe you can create a fair society. But remember, Derek, no one wants to stay here. We all want to get to UK. Let's get you to bed.

A CRS Officer in full riot gear enters and pins a piece of paper to a wall. Only Safi seems to notice.

Derek No, no, no. There will soon come a time when everything is threatened. When the whole idea might be destroyed. When they come –

Mohammed Come on.

Derek And they will come. We have to know what we are defending. What we stand for. Safi!

Safi I'm sorry, I wasn't listening.

Mohammed takes Derek off.

It's one thing ending a year in the Jungle. It's another starting a new one.

Omar enters.

Omar My friend.

Safi What?

Omar Your coat.

Safi I don't have anything else.

Omar I think I die tonight.

Safi stares blankly. He takes his coat off and gives it to Omar. He stands in the freezing cold in nothing but a T-shirt.
Outside Norullah's tent.

Norullah (*Pashto*) I can see a big road. With tall houses made of bricks. Grey, with shiny front doors painted black. Cars driving past. It's noisy. There are lots of lights. Lots of people. Men and women, yes. Everyone is wearing a hat . . . And . . . Wait. (*To Okot.*) Okot!

What?

Norullah What is in London?

Okot Big Ben . . .

Norullah (*Pashto*) I can see Big Ben. Wait. (*To Okot, in English.*) What does it look like?

Okot It's big.

Norullah (*Pashto*) It's big. Wait. (*To Okot, in English.*) How big?

Okot I don't know. Big!

Norullah (*Pashto*) I don't know how big! (*To Okot, in English.*) What does it look like?

Okot What do you mean? It's a fucking clock. Who are you talking to?

Norullah (*Pashto*) It's a clock. Yeah, big clock. (*To Okot, in English.*) More things from UK.

Okot London Eye?

Norullah (*Pashto*) London Eye. (*To Okot, in English.*) What the fuck is that?

Okot Big wheel to see the city . . . I don't know!

Norullah Fucking big clock and big wheel? That all?

Okot Chelsea Football, Buckingham Palace, London Bridge.

Norullah (*Pashto.*) Chelsea Football. Buckingham Palace. London Bridge. Yes, I can see it all out my window.

Okot Who are you talking to?

Norullah (*Pashto*) That's my friend. I am living with him. He's called Okot.

Okot Who is it?

Norullah Shhh. My mother.

Okot You're talking to your mother?

Norullah (*Pashto*) Yes, Mother, he is a very nice English boy.

Okot What are you saying?

Norullah (*Pashto*) Good parents, yes.

Okot Norullah!

Norullah Shhh. I tell her I am in UK.

Okot What?!

Norullah Otherwise she is worry about me!

Okot Oh, fuck, man. No, you need to tell her the truth.

He goes to get the phone.

Norullah (*Pashto*) Mum, I've got to go. Okot is calling for me. Yes, I love you. Love my aunties, love my cousins, I love you, I miss you, I call you.

He puts the phone down.

Okot What the fuck?

Norullah Is mothers, man! She fucking calling all day, ask me all time: I am safe? I am safe?

Okot You can't lie to her like that.

Norullah But she just go crazy if she know I am in Jungle. Yes, my mother! I am so safe! I say I am with my friend, best friend, UK friend! We is look after each other. She is saying, you eat food, you warm, you live house –

Okot She'll find out.

Norullah I send photos from website and say is my house, is Queen of UK house from my phone. She cannot believe! Oh, Mother, London so fucking big. I love London fucking so much, Mother.

Okot How long have you been saying that?

Norullah Fucking months, man. What you say to yours?

Okot I haven't spoken to her.

Norullah Mothers going crazy for us, I think! I am in school! I am in house! I am in family! I am in new life, Mother! Don't cry, Mother! Don't cry, Mother! I love you too, Mother! I love you too!

Pause. Suddenly he breaks down in tears.

I miss my mother.

Okot comforts him, Norullah cannot control himself.

I want to see my mother! I want my mother.

Okot cradles him.

Okot You will see her one day.

Norullah What if I don't?

Okot You will. It won't be long . . . Hey, listen to this . . .

He sings Sudanese song, still holding Norullah.

Norullah What is this?

Okot My mother used to sing to me.

Norullah What it mean?

Okot It means, I love you. Don't worry. Everything is going to be OK.

Okot finishes the song.

OK, I have an idea. We're going to go and try.

Norullah Salar says no try.

Okot Fuck Salar. We try. Come on.

They leave.

Beth Safi? Safi.

Ali's caravan.

Ali Why are you here, Beth?

Beth He's called Okot.

Ali In the Jungle.

Beth I don't really have time –

Ali I like to know people I'm going to work with.

Safi Beth runs the school.

Ali I've heard about the school. You are a charity person then.

Beth No.

Ali No?

Beth It's not charity.

Ali What is it?

Beth It's not anything. It's not a choice. It's just what I'm doing.

Ali You didn't think, 'I'll build a school'?

Beth I didn't think I would come here at all.

Ali How long have you been here?

Safi Five months.

Ali Months!

Beth Not as long as Okot.

Ali Do you know how many people I see come for one day? You have moved in. You have become a refugee. We are very similar.

Beth You're a smuggler.

Safi Beth, you can't –

Ali No, Safi, it's fine. You British always use this word. Like we are in the business of moving tobacco.

Beth What are you?

Ali I am freedom fighter. Peshmerga, the Army of Kurdistan. You know what this word means? Those who face death. Everyone here has lost their home, but we have never had one. This is our fight, and we find no help from your governments. You are happy to see refugees die as long as he is wearing new shoes. I help them find a home. I fight for real freedom.

He looks into her eyes.

You would do the same.

Beth And take their money.

Ali You are very suspicious of me.

Beth I think this whole situation is because of you.

Ali Smugglers? I am one man, helps some rich families. I make money, yes, but most of it goes back to Erbil for the fight against Daesh. Yes. Once I was the only way a man could ever dream of arriving on your shore. Now, he opens the map on his phone, zooms out, and thinks, 'It's not too far. It's close to enough to *walk*.' And he sets off on the journey of his life. It is not about this border. It's the border in here – (*Taps his head.*) It is gone now. Tell me about Okot.

Beth What do you want to know?

Ali Black boy?

Beth Sudanese.

Ali Child?

Beth Seventeen.

Ali Why him?

Beth Do I need a reason?

Ali There are many boys in the Jungle.

Beth He doesn't have anyone else. Are you going to help or not?

Ali This doesn't happen, a British volunteer coming to me. For a friend of Safi's . . . €1,000.

Safi A good price.

Beth Thank you.

Ali Thank me when I have helped him.

Ali hands his phone to her. She types her number in.

I'll call you. One week, maybe, one month, maybe.

Beth What will happen?

Ali We give him an onion. We put him in a box. And I'll shut the door myself. How does that sound?

Beth An onion?

Ali For the guard dogs. The smell keeps them away. I like you, Beth. You are trying to understand. But you can't. The world is different now. It will never be the same. I will give your friend his freedom.

Beth Let's go.

Safi I'll stay.

Beth OK.

She exits.

Ali Impressive girl.

Safi Is that true about the onion?

Ali Safi, I'm expensive for a reason.

Safi You will help her, won't you?

Ali Where is your coat?

Safi I left it . . .

Ali You gave it away.

Safi I didn't.

Ali You will freeze to death. When are you going to stop this?

Safi Stop what?

Ali This act. The man who helps.

Safi I don't know what you are talking about.

Ali Yes, you do. How are you, Safi?

Safi How am I? My feet are changing colour.

He laughs, almost hysterically.

I feel . . .

Ali Go on.

Safi Things have changed here. People are mad, all the time. Problems, questions. A man pulled a knife on me because I wouldn't get him a house!

Ali You look tired.

Safi I feel angry.

Ali You should.

Safi I am fleeing too. I have horrors. They have no idea of the pictures in my mind.

Ali No one cares about you. Don't you think it might be time?

Pause.

You are the only person who would find this decision difficult.

Pause.

Safi I have to leave.

Safi I will kill myself by staying.

Ali No guilt.

Safi No.

Ali You have been a good man.

Safi Oh fuck, no.

Ali And now it is your time.

Safi I can't begin another year here, Ali. You understand that. Don't you?

*Okot and Norullah sit on a bridge over the
motorway. Lorries speed past beneath them.*

Okot This is the game. You watch for lorry coming. You see it drive. It comes close to bridge, then jump. We don't need dugar. We don't need smuggler. We don't need Beth. We do it together.

Norullah It's really far.

Okot You are big man.

Norullah I'm not.

Okot You are not bambino.

Norullah No . . .

Okot You can do it.

Norullah But what if we miss?

Okot We won't.

Norullah Then we die!

Okot I've done this before. I know it can work.

Norullah Okot, I think I no want to –

Okot Your mother thinks you're in UK, yes?

Norullah Yes.

Okot She tell you to go UK.

Norullah Yes.

Okot Only UK.

Norullah Yes.

Okot So let's go!

Norullah But this is crazy!

Okot It's not crazy.

Norullah I know what is crazy, and this is fucking crazy.

Okot Listen to me, Norullah. You don't want to be left on your own here, OK? You need to get out of Jungle.

Norullah We should talk to Miss Beth.

Okot She is not going to help you! You have to help yourself! There, that lorry coming now. Are you ready?

Norullah I don't know . . .

Okot We do this!

Norullah Okot . . .

Okot For UK. For dream.

Norullah No . . .

Okot Three . . .

Norullah Please...

Okot Two . . .

Norullah Oh, fucking shit...

Okot One . . .

A lorry speeds by below. The rain stops.

SEVEN
THE GREAT MOVE

A crisis meeting in Salar's restaurant.

Derek 'The regular incursions of migrants on to the road is posing a threat to public safety.' We need translators. Where is Safi?

Sam The notice gives police the authority to clear a hundred-metre strip of land around the entire perimeter of the Jungle.

Salar They are evicting us.

Sam It's a partial relocation, if we want it to be.

Mohammed What is in the eviction zone?

Sam (*showing them a map*) Eight hundred houses. Two thousand people.

Ali The Kurdish church.

Paula The family area.

Mohammed When?

Sam Friday.

Boxer It's Monday!

Mohammed Is it legal?

114

Sam Under state of emergency law, yes.

Paula Fuck's sake!

Derek We have a choice. Co-operate with the authorities, relocate everyone before Friday. Or resist. You have to decide. We will support the choice you make.

Salar has been studying the map.

Salar My restaurant! They destroy my restaurant!

Sam (*to Henri*) Why didn't you tell me?

Henri I told you what I could.

Sam Two thousand people! What am I supposed to do?

Henri Relocate them before the police do it.

Sam In three days? Where? The camp is full. There's talk of resisting.

Henri Resist the CRS?

Sam They are sick of being moved!

Henri What do you want me to say?

Sam I need to know this won't happen again in two weeks' time.

Henri It won't.

Sam There are no more evictions planned.

Henri No.

Sam Promise me.

Henri There are no more evictions planned.

Norullah (*to Okot*) Jungle finished.

He pulls up a huge dead bird. It's beautiful. A snow crane. Long, thin, orange legs. Its neck dangles down almost touching the mud.

Okot What's that?

Norullah Bird.

Okot What bird?

Norullah I don't know. We have in Afghanistan.

Okot What's it doing here?

Norullah Lost. Dunno.

Okot You found it?

Norullah I killed it.

Okot How?

Norullah You want to see?

He takes out a gun.

Okot Shit. Put it away, put it away.

Norullah puts it away, as Okot checks that no one is around.

Let me see. Where did you get it?

Norullah Bought it. Wanna try?

Mohammed (*to the meeting*) Sudan want to relocate.

Helene Eritrea.

Yasin Iraq.

Omid Iran.

Derek We will do everything we can to help.

Salar No. The Afghan people wish to resist.

Mohammed Think about this, Salar.

Salar I have.

Ali If Afghanistan resists, then so does Kurdistan. We stand with you, Salar.

Mohammed We have escaped war. We do not need more!

Sam takes Derek aside.

Sam We have to stop this!

Derek We can't force them.

Sam We can. And we should.

Derek How can you know what is right for them?

Sam We know what the CRS do!

Derek They have every right to resist the destruction of their home.

Sam Their houses won't be destroyed if we move them!

Derek Their home, Sam! Not houses! This is bigger than houses, bigger than the Jungle. I'm sorry to say it, but you don't understand that, and you don't know what it means to resist.

Sam Because I'm young.

Derek Because nothing you hold dear has ever been threatened.

Sam Fuck you, Derek.

Derek These people have lost everything.

Sam And we have a duty to keep them safe.

Derek Some fights are greater than individual safety.

Sam This is not a good place, Derek! It isn't something to be preserved.

Derek The Diggers, the Chartists, the Suffragettes, Greenham Common.

Sam Oh, come on.

Derek You stand on the shoulders of giants, and you don't even know who they are. These people are the strangers of the world. Bombed, abused, humiliated.

Sam I hadn't noticed.

Derek This might be their time.

Henri (*to Sam*) Sam, you're running out of time.

Sam (*to the meeting*) The area will be cleared. That's not a choice. The choice is by who. You can let the police do it. They'd like nothing more. They'll come in with batons and tear gas. They'll destroy everything. Or we do it ourselves. No one gets hurt. We decide.

Mohammed Let's take a moment for thought.

On the beach, Okot holds the gun.

Norullah Both hands. Hold it steady. Point. Don't press.

Okot It's really heavy.

Norullah That's why it cost a lot of money.

Okot What should I shoot?

Norullah What do you want to shoot?

Okot I don't want to shoot a bird.

Norullah Shoot a stone. Shoot the sea.

Okot I'm going to shoot UK. You see the white cliffs. Fuck you, UK.

Okot shoots, recoils.

Safi Shit.

Norullah Give me, give me. (*Shooting until it's out of bullets.*) FUCK YOU, UK!

Safi Give me the gun.

Norullah WHY MY MOTHER SAY GO UK?

Safi Norullah, give me the gun.

Norullah WHY I AM HERE?

Safi Give me the gun!

Norullah WHY YOU NOT WANT ME?

Okot Do you think they reach?

Norullah Definitely.

Sam (*to Salar*) I can move your restaurant, Salar. Tomorrow. Wherever you want. It will be exactly the same, I promise you.

Salar I will not move.

Sam If you resist, people will die.

Salar It is their will.

Sam So persuade them otherwise.

Salar I cannot force them.

Sam You are their leader!

Salar Just as you cannot force me.

Sam How much have you told them?

Salar Are you accusing me of lying to my people?

Sam They will lose!

Salar 1839. 1888. 2001.

Sam What?

Salar Karz. My village in Afghanistan.

Sam Please.

Salar You know nothing of our struggle, Sam. For you, this is a good chance. For us, it is our life.

Salar You know nothing of our struggle. For you, this is a good chance. For us, it is our life.

Sam I know I can leave when I want. I know I could be at home with my family. I know I could be anywhere but the fucking Jungle. I know that, but I'm not. I am here. I'm still here. I'm still here.

Salar I built this restaurant with my hands. Every piece of wood, everything you see, I found. It has been a roof over our heads through rain, wind and fire. It has been our safety and refuge. It is our home. It is our heart. I will not move.

Mohammed takes his hands.

Mohammed We looked into each other's eyes on the day we arrived and made a promise.

Salar No, Mohammed –

Mohammed Look at me. We promised to stand together. Your restaurant is not this land or this wood. It is us. You are my friend, and I love you. We must stand together now.

Sam Salar, I think I can persuade the authorities to protect your restaurant. If I can do this, will you support me with the relocation of houses? (*To Henri.*) We begin tomorrow morning. I still don't know if I can relocate everyone in three days.

Henri If we see evidence of co-operation, the police will hold back.

Sam The restaurant, the Afghan Flag. You have to promise me it won't be touched. It's the only way I can persuade them to move.

Henri I'm sure we can come to an arrangement.

Safi Wednesday.

Sam (*to everyone*) We're moving Eritreans north of the women and children's centre. Boxer's been up all night in the digger clearing land. Well done, Boxer.

Boxer Wired as a ferret on Ritalin but I got another three days in me. Right, you need nine people to pick up a shelter. Four on corners, four on sides, one person spotting and guiding.

Mohammed Derek will be leading community liaison.

Derek Everyone is going to have new neighbours. If there are problems, speak to me.

Paula The centre's open twenty-four hours. Special attention to the kids, please. This will be hugely traumatic for them.

Helene The church serves food and drink for everyone who needs it.

Mohammed We stand together.

Salar God grant us great fortune.

All Inshallah.

Sam We have three days. This is our time. Let's show them how we do things here.

The Great Move begins.

Okot (*to Norullah*) Why did you buy it?

Norullah Defence. France police destroy my house? Bang. Salar makes me go shop? Bang.

Okot Salar is not a good man.

Norullah No good man here. Bang. Bang. Bang. Fucking police! Fucking Jungle! Fucking fence! Fucking France! Fucking Afghanistan! Fucking rain! Fucking cold! Fucking rats! Fucking mud! Fucking sick! Sick of being bambino.

Okot We'll be in UK soon.

Norullah Fucking UK! No chance! They hate us. We're going to die here.

Safi Thursday.

Sam (*to everyone*) Afghans west of the dome. (*To Henri.*) You can see we're moving.

Henri I'll speak with my superiors.

Sam They have to delay.

Henri I'll speak with them.

Salar (*to Sam*) My restaurant?

Sam (*to Henri*) And the restaurant?

Henri It can stay.

Sam (*to Salar*) I have assurances. The restaurant won't be touched.

Ali (*to Beth*) Tomorrow night. A lorry park near Guînes. Eight p.m. Don't be late.

Beth We won't.

Ali One more thing. The price is up.

Beth We had an agreement.

Ali The border has changed. There are more police. €500.

Beth You say you aren't a smuggler.

Ali Eight p.m. Don't be late.

   Beth leaves.

Eight p.m., Safi.

Safi Friday.

Sam (*to everyone*) Kurdistan. Families to the north, men by the lake. (*To Henri.*) I'm nearly done. Tell me the police won't come in at dawn.

Henri They're happy with your co-operation. They are not monsters, Sam.

Okot (*to Norullah*) I have to go.

Norullah Where?

Pause.

Where are you going?

Okot I don't know.

Norullah You leave me?

Okot I don't know.

Norullah What the fuck?

Okot I don't know!

Norullah What about me?

Okot I don't know what's happening! I didn't ask her to do anything!

Norullah You can't leave me here! Don't leave me in the Jungle! Please.

Okot I won't leave you!

Norullah starts screaming, and runs.

Norullah!

The roof of the restaurant is stripped back, revealing the huge claws of a bulldozer descending. Sam runs underneath it.

Sam No! Stop!

*Salar joins him. Mohammed, Paula, Derek, Boxer,
and Helene, who holds a huge crucifix high in the air,
shouting 'Lord Have Mercy'.*

*All the residents and volunteers join, their bodies
a shield.*

You cannot touch the restaurant!

CRS Officer We have orders.

Sam Your orders are wrong.

CRS Officer Don't understand you, boy! This is France,
you speak French.

Sam Look at yourselves! This is not France!

Henri (*to Sam*) I know! I'm sorry! The message did not
get through –

Sam You promised me!

Henri Let me make a call –

Sam The restaurant cannot be touched.

Henri It is a mistake, that's all.

Sam Will there be another eviction?

Henri I have told you. No.

Safi This is when my mind becomes muddy. There was a
deal, an agreement, that a church could remain. Or was
it a mosque? I know it wasn't a restaurant.

There were two churches.

The first one the authorities tried to destroy, we
worked together to move it. A whole church in one hour.
I will never forget the sight of the pastor holding an
almighty crucifix in the air, wailing as his congregation
wept on the floor beside him.

We saved it. Only for a while, but we saved it.

Or the second church, the other time the authorities
tried to demolish, it was the Eritrean church, this time

the congregation came outside with all the iconography and art and they prayed together, loudly, defiantly, into the mouth of the bulldozer.

These were places of worship.

This restaurant. Where we are sat. It was really many restaurants. Cafés, shops, places. Each of them a Jungle. And in this story, in my head, this restaurant is saved. It is a story of great hope because it has to be. Looking back, there is no other way. This restaurant, in this moment, is Afghanistan. And the people inside it, us, from Sudan, Eritrea, Syria, Iran, Iraq, Somalia, Britain, Germany, American, and some from France, yes, held hands to defend it. They believed in it.

Great is the hope that makes man cross borders. Great is the hope that keeps us alive.

Beth finds Okot.

Beth Quick, or we'll be late.

Okot Norullah is gone!

Beth We have to go now. You'll be in the UK tonight. Can you believe it?

Okot I can't leave him here.

Beth Don't worry about Norullah. I'll find him. This is your only chance.

The lorry park.

Safi My story of the Jungle ends with an onion.

Beth gives Ali money, which he counts.

Beth (*to Okot*) Here's a bag. There are two phones. A torch, hat, gloves, I don't know how cold it will get.

Safi If he takes you to a refrigerated lorry do not get inside.

Beth Listen to Safi. Plenty of water, some biscuits, money. First thing you do when you arrive is find a police station. Tell them your story, exactly what you told me. Tell them you're a child. Tell them you want to claim asylum.

She holds him tight and doesn't let go.

You're going to start a new life, Okot. All of this will be finished. It won't be you.

Okot It will never leave.

Beth Yes, it will. Everything is new now. This is the hope.

Ali We have to go.

Beth can't let him go.

Safi He'll be fine.

She leaves.

Ali Quick.

Okot goes to Ali. Safi goes to follow.

Not you, Safi. (*To Okot.*) Wait down there.

He directs Okot off in one direction.

Safi What's going on?

Ali I only have one.

Safi What do you mean?

Ali I only have one onion.

He holds it out. Safi considers, walks towards him.

Safi I'm sorry.

He takes the onion.

Ali No guilt.

Ali leaves.

Safi I felt every vibration as the lorry travelled over every bump and hole in the road. I heard every noise. I panicked every time the lorry stopped and thought it must be the end.

For eighteen hours I stayed quiet, with my onion, hardly breathing. Then the doors opened. I will never forget the face of the man who opened the box. 'Quickly, mate. You're in England.'

I came to a place called Maidstone and found a police station. My name is Safi Al-Hussain. I have fled Syria. I would like to claim asylum in UK. And then I handed her my onion.

Salar's restaurant.

Salar They wanted a fight! They wanted to come with their batons and bulldozers. They wanted to destroy the Afghan Flag. But we showed them who we are!

Sam Two thousand people. Three days. And we have a promise from the authorities there will be no more evictions.

Derek Yes, yes, it's all very exciting. But we have a lot to get through. First on the agenda, Paula, I know you have some more good news. Translations, please.

Paula The Home Office lost in court . . . We won. The first child under Dublin III arrives at London St Pancras tomorrow. We are going to get every child to safety.

Derek Alright, very good. Let's plough on. What's next?

Sam We're creating a new area by the lake. Quadrant 7. Building begins tomorrow.

Derek Helene?

Helene The church is open. We have mass at ten a.m.! Thanks God!

Derek Boxer.

Boxer Running a carpentry workshop. We're making house numbers and street signs, name your own street. We're going to make this place look pretty.

Derek The school, Beth?

Beth English lessons tomorrow morning. Arts and crafts in the afternoon. If anyone sees Norullah, please let me know.

Salar Tell him I need a hundred chickens and six sacks of rice! The restaurant is open. Any problems with building, we have sleeping places.

Derek OK, good, good. What's next?

Safi The southern half of the camp was evicted four weeks later.

In October, the north.

And the Jungle was gone.

Now, fields of yellow rape, six feet high, grow in the sand where the Jungle once was. Apart from small footprints, where nothing grows. Where the church stood. Mosques. A restaurant.

Thank you for your hospitality.

I hope one day to return to Aleppo. When I do, you are all very welcome to visit.

But to those who were our friends, who are not here now, we pray for you. We thank you. We love you. May peace be with you. And Allah grant you safety and comfort.

Beth enters with piles of donations.

There are nearly a thousand refugees still living in Calais today. The police prevent any building. Any sign that things might grow again. Volunteers distribute what little they have. Their vans give out meals in car parks, roads, wherever they can.

Beth.

Beth Still here. In Calais. I never left.

A boy enters. He looks like Okot.

Al-Sadig Salutations.

Beth turns.

Beth Okot?

Al-Sadig My name is Al-Sadig. I am one five. I just arrived.

Beth It's good to meet you, Al-Sadig. My name is Beth. I am two zero. Now, it's very dangerous for you to be here. The police are all around this area, and they're not as friendly as they used to be. They come at this time every night so we need to be quick. I think there are some nice Sudanese men in the woods nearby. I can take you to them. But first, can I ask you a favour? I need your help.

She gives him lots of donations to carry, and they walk off together.

The End.